THE
SAILING LIFE

Other books by Bob Bitchin

A Brotherhood of Outlaws
Biker
Emerald Bay
Letters from the LOST SOUL

THE
SAILING LIFE

BOB BITCHIN

S
SHERIDAN HOUSE

First published 2006 by
Sheridan House Inc.
145 Palisade Street
Dobbs Ferry, NY 10522
www.sheridanhouse.com

This book is based on articles previously published in
Latitudes & Attitudes.

Library of Congress Cataloging-in-Publication Data

Bitchin, Bob.
  The sailing life / Bob Bitchin.
     p. cm.
  ISBN 1-57409-221-9 (alk. paper)
  1. Sailing—Anecdotes. 2. Bitchin, Bob. I. Title.
  GV811.B48 2006
  797.124—dc22

                                     2005032226

ISBN 1-57409-221-9

Printed in the United States of America

Contents

Foreword by Tania Aebi   ix

Introduction   xix

PART 1
THE LEARNING CURVE   1
It is not the place, it is the time   3
Love/hate relationship   6
Preparation, perspiration and luck   10
Rules . . . we don't need no rules!   13
Too safe?   16
Nautical history, who needs it?   19
Life cycles   22
The crew of the UNICORN   25
The best anchor ever made   28
Regulations   32
Un-civilized?   36
Sailors are weird   39
Hard-fought victory   42
Thanks, Captain Olsen   45

PART 2
CRUISING   49
What is a cruiser?   51
Charts   54

Mysterious sailor   57
Fade to black . . .   60
Blush on the rose refit   64
The perfect cruising boat   67
Depth of feelings   70
And there you are   73
Peter Island boat   77
Joys of varnishing   80
Taking responsibility   83
Have what you want?   86
When to fly the Jolly Roger   89
Life out there is a dream   92

PART 3
ATTITUDE   97
    Attitude   99
    Sailors have more fun than people   101
    You know you are a cruiser   104
    Reaping the rewards   107
    XY chromosome   110
    The barroom advice   113
    Wrong Bay Bob   116
    Ready to go?   119
    The third day   122
    Saltwater cures all   125
    The two happiest days   128
    Finding a way   131
    Think you're smart?   134
    Life is maintenance   137

PART 4
LIVING THE DREAM   141
  Enjoy the moment   143
  Living the dream   146
  Pearls before swine   149
  A voyage is like life   152
  Quiet time   155
  The perfect moment   158
  The dream is still there   162
  Adjust the sail   165
  No matter where you go   168
  The little moments   171
  A cruisers' beach party   174

PART 5
THE BEST OF *LATITUDES & ATTITUDES*
EDITORIALS   177
  No explanation   179
  Cruising, what a concept   182
  Got milk?   185
  Slay the dragon   188
  Official millennium editorial   191
  Sexist, me?   194
  The sacrifices I make   198
  You gotta do what you want   201

Bob, a foreword.

>———►◄———

*J*uly 2005. I was three days away from wrapping up two years of intensive schoolwork and thinking I could take a break from all the writing when the e-mail from Bob came in. "Could you please write a foreword? I figure you can whip out 1200-1500 words in a couple of hours," he wrote, always the optimist, not to mention the kind of guy who regularly whips out 1200-1500 words in a couple of hours, while holding a conversation, or sitting at a chart table between two islands. He can do it after a day spent in a boat show booth, or in a hotel room on the road, whatever it takes to pull together the next issue of *Latitudes & Attitudes*. When he isn't writing, he's talking to people. When he isn't talking to people, he's talking into a tape recorder or video camera. When he isn't talking into a tape recorder or video camera, he's eating. Then he sleeps, wakes up, eats, and starts all over again. If all of life is a stage, his setting is the world, and with all that writing, talking, recording, and eating, he is out in it, big, front, and center. The production revolves around him with the leading lady, Jody, and all the other major and minor characters on the sidelines, running his businesses, his supporting cast and stage crew. And, through it all, he keeps writing. He's a writing machine.

"Yeah right. Not me." I wrote back, immediately answering his e-mail, the only writing I do painlessly, and always the realist, especially in regards to my writing and time management and wanting to do a good job for him. At first, I asked for a couple of weeks, not wanting to ask for too much. So what if my summer was busy? You want to talk busy, look at him. Then his publisher assured me I had a couple of months, so I figured I'd have plenty of time to figure out an angle on Bob from which 1200-1500 words would easily flow. Like he does on a daily basis, I'd find an idea, and be able to focus directly on it and whip something out.

But, the words never, ever flow for me, and between renovating a house, taking care of my kids, and hosting the rest of my extended family and friends for half the summer, I just barely managed to meet the magazine's three monthly column deadlines while this one loomed over them all. I mean, I sat down and "whipped" out all kinds of snippets, bits of Bob, but it's not easy to pull together such a huge guy, his story, and what he represents in words he hasn't used. What about Bob?

There are many reasons why a person would buy a boat and cast off the docklines. Everyone has a story, and Bob's is all about trading in the life of a biker (except for the tattoos plastering his body) for that of a sailor. When he exchanged his Harley for the LOST SOUL, he never looked back as he and Jody sailed into their future of building dreams and a friendly magazine for cruisers. When I met them, they were into their second year of publishing, and seven years later, *Latitudes & Attitudes* has 70,000 monthly readers who love its carefree optimism and insight into another way of life among regular folks who live on and around sailboats. And, for these readers, Bob's constant message is a theme about attitude, how it is the only difference between an ordeal and an adventure.

Before ever being introduced to Bob, I already knew how to appreciate the type. He's cut from the same mold as my father who has a sign taped to the front door of his home: dream-to-reality conversion specialist. My father earned himself a reputation, not as the successful, hardworking entrepreneur he was, but as the guy who offered his daughter a choice: either go to college, or sail around the world alone, and write about it. Not quite the Hell's Angels, but still pretty dramatic. The way I see it, Bob and my father belong to the post-war generation, where focused determination and abnormal amounts of self-confidence enabled them to rise to the surface. They give substance to the word entrepreneur, a person who organizes and manages a business undertaking, assuming the risk for the sake of a profit. But for them, risk and profit don't always have to be of the financial sort. It's also about taking risks to enhance the quality of life and experience by taking alternative routes, and to succeed by sheer force of will.

Each guy, in his own, highly individualistic way, is a tour de force, grabbing life by the horns with boundless optimism, living each day fully, always thinking, cooking up plans, starting projects, and sweeping all their people along in their slipstreams. And unless part of the show is involving them in some kind of deliberate trial of suffering—Bob's sleepless nonstop cross-country Harley ride to earn a land speed record, or my dad's camel caravan ride across the desert—they do nothing without thinking ahead about the dinner table, where they can bring their indomitable attitude to family and friends. Then, after that, they sit down to write.

September 2005. One hazy, Indian summer Monday, Bob and Jody were on their way to my house, and here I must stress that, for me, it is always Bob *and* Jody. Without one, there is no other, and if Bob reminds me of a father, Jody is like a sister. I know her status as his wife ought to make her like a mother, but it isn't like that. She's a sister, a girlfriend, Bob's main pillar of support and her devotion to him is beautiful. I'm glad they have each other. I was so happy to be hosting them for once, to be able to show off the place I came home to after each time they hosted me with souvlaki in Greece, roast chicken and vodka cranberries in New Zealand, and all kinds of other meals in California. Because I've spent time with them on the water and at their home, I know, more than anything else, Bob is a big guy because he likes to eat and Jody likes to cook. So, when I got up early to prepare the kids for school, I also began to prepare our lunch.

I'd received an e-mail from Jody, sent from their office in a Californian oceanfront resort. While reading it, I could imagine well the *Latitudes & Attitudes* headquarters overlooking the marina where they and others on the magazine staff kept their boats, and their upstairs apartment with panoramic windows overlooking the docks and barking seals on one side, and the entire Pacific Ocean on the other. Several weeks earlier, I'd stayed with them during the magazine's advanced cruising seminar, the annual weekend organized to help future cruisers gather information. During past seminars, I'd bunked in LOST SOUL's forward queen suite, but this year, she was undergoing a major refit and termite extermination, and Bob and Jody had moved into this apartment with Hollywood views. Portofino Marina and its environs, twenty minutes from LAX, is the only California I know well enough to like. Aside from beaches, bathers, surfers, piers, and fishermen to watch, Bob and Jody and the family who keeps the Bitchin fleet afloat are there—Woody, Sue and Mike, Charky, Cheryl, Tom and Lynn, are just part of the tableau of characters, old friends, and histories that come together to color this cool Redondo Beach scene.

But, I think I have a cool scene, too, even if it's way inland, nowhere near the sea, boats, and sailors I write about. For years—and it's funny how fast they accumulate—I'd been telling Bob and Jody, "It's just a day trip up to me from the Newport Boat Show." They attend it every September, and this time, they accepted the invitation and were coming. They'd be driving up on Monday, Jody wrote four days earlier, and were planning to arrive around midday. After writing back with directions, I never heard another word. With them, no news is no news. If they said they were coming, they would.

As I spent the pre-dawn hours making the boys breakfasts and lunches while they practiced piano and squabbled before heading off to school, I cut, mixed, and popped a blueberry buckle into the oven. When the kids were gone, I picked onions, carrots, and herbs from the garden, and washed and cut them up with a chicken from the freezer, one we'd raised the previous summer. Oven and stovetop loaded, cats, rabbits, laying hens and this year's batch of meat chickens all fed, I went down to the worksite.

●◦●

Priming pieces of window trim that had been cut too many times because mitering can be tricky, involving extra trips to the building supply store for more wood, where the people are nice, at a price, I thought about Bob and Jody and the mountain home they were building. "It's almost impossible to get out of a building supply store without spending anything," Bob had said in his office as he clicked through pictures of their new spread. We talked less boat, and more about foundations, fixtures, countertop choices, views, remoteness, and wildlife, the black bear I saw out at my chicken coop, the 800-pound bronze bear statue he's erecting outside their front door. Like me, they're building in a place others call "the middle of nowhere," which is part of the appeal.

I made a list of things to get on the next trip to town, a list I wouldn't have when I got there, because I was too busy remembering other things, like getting food into the oven on time and watching the clock. When the time came, I put away the paintbrush, returned home to put the chicken and beets into the oven and Jody called. They were about 90 minutes away.

"Don't eat," I said, noting 90 minutes is plenty of cooking time for a good meal to be ready. I wanted them to like it here, starting with the food. They did.

I gave them a tour of the property, and in the woods, we talked trees. In the house we talked construction. Over lunch we talked recipes and boat shows. I introduced them to my boys and to my father in his empire up the road, the meeting of the kings. We filled their tank with gas at the Crossroads Trading Post, where proprietor Joe with a Harley talked bikes with Bob, and fifteen minutes later, crossing the lawn to my house, Bob was talking into his tape recorder, a reminder to send Joe a copy of his biker book, *Brotherhood of Outlaws*. Then, we stood beside the chicken coop and talked some more about heating systems, gardening, wells, and a magazine about mountain home lifestyles. Yes, it actually came up. One day, having spread the sailing life message, he just might write his last sailing editorial and start back up with the mountains. And why not? If anybody can do it, Bob can.

October 2005. I kept thinking about attitude and the difference between ordeal and adventure over the summer, while agonizing over ideas, fact, and sentiment. Then, when life crowded in, I ran off and avoided wrapping up Bob until the last minute, which is now, one more in seven years of Bob deadlines. By giving me a column, he got me writing about sailing again, regularly, and whenever our wakes have crossed, I've had a deadline looming, for him. But so has he, many more, yet unlike many of us, he always knows exactly what he wants to say and gets it out ahead of time, like my youngest boy who is always ahead a couple of days with his homework. I don't know where they get it from, and such self-discipline and self-awareness is downright inspirational.

Editorials, articles, advertisements, boat shows, cars, trucks, containers, shipments, a boat, an office, shops, real estate, the house he and Jody are building, decisions to make constantly, and he keeps writing, spreading this can-do attitude through his words. He doesn't just talk the talk, he walks the walk, except if it involves actually walking, because he's not into exercise. It's one of the things he delegates to Jody, which is when she and I get to hang out and talk about Bob's world from a girlie perspective. Other than riding the walk, though, he's a good example.

Since I started writing for *Latitudes & Attitudes*, people have asked me questions. An e-mail comes in. "Where the hell did he get a name like Bob Bitchin?" the writer asks.

I reply, "Bitchin is Bob's biker name, back from the days when he rode a hog and was Evel Knievel's body guard." I've seen the footage. From those biker days, he holds onto the tag name and video clips he can show guests on a huge-screen TV with a remote he knows how to use. Back then, he also wrote *Brotherhood of Outlaws*, and started a biker magazine *and* a tattoo magazine. I've never ridden a hog, and the closest I've ever come to the Hell's Angels was walking past their East Village hangout as a kid, then driving once through Sturgis a week before the rally, now watching them roar past my home on their yearly pilgrimage to Laconia, and finally, reading the *Electric Kool Aid Acid Test* several months ago. I was invited onto his stage only after he sold the biker mag to get the boat, then started the sailing rag.

Another popular question is: "Do those guys really party all the time?" The casual, fun-loving message in the magazine does have a party-like atmosphere. But if you log on to bobbitchin.com, you will be greeted by the words, "Welcome to ego hell." Does that sound like a party? So begins Bob's online introduction to himself, a self-proclaimed "idiot." It's true. He also calls himself an idiot. Then, he goes on to admit the site only exists because of crass commercialism, that he is there ready to sell whatever you want to buy, just so he can continue on with his life of decadence

and poisoning thousands of minds worldwide, *Latitudes &
Attitudes* being the brainwashing vehicle. He summarizes
his idyllic childhood in one sentence before continuing
with more about being a biker dude, and the growth of a
writerly career promoting a lifestyle on two wheels until it
led to the helm of LOST SOUL, and a new magazine promoting the lifestyle of the sailor. He calls his biker years "the
degenerate period," but hey, wait a second. I'm sorry, but
recreational drugs, pretty women, and tattoos do not always
a degenerate make, Bob. I've known degenerates, and they
don't accomplish much.

Maybe he was a weekend party animal, but the rest of
the time, reddened or not, his eyes were square on the ball.
A guy who starts three magazines, lobbies for motorcycle
legislation, writes books, organizes and sponsors rallies, is
still alive after putting half a million miles on his Harley,
and has a wife who loves him, many loyal and old friends
and a diligently down-to-earth staff does not have the de-
graded morals and intellect, or the time, to be a degenerate.
Not in my book. And with all that on the burners, he didn't
have the time it takes to lead a double life, either. No, I
think I'd call this kind of person a mover and a shaker, a
leader.

In the final analysis, then, with *Latitudes & Attitudes*,
and his huge personality, degenerate or not, Bob has managed to bring a breath of honest fresh air to the cruising way
of life at a time when all the joy and laughter was being
suppressed by all kinds of seriousness and expertise in
other sailing publications. It's okay to be irreverent. It's
okay to make mistakes, as long as you learn from them.

We're all flawed and nobody can know everything, but so what? Should that stop us from having fun with turning our dreams into reality? *Latitudes & Attitudes* broke the snooty, yachtie stereotype and helped to make the cruising lifestyle feel accessible to the mainstream, not just to specialists. Bob is definitely not mainstream, but he knows optimism is universal to those who are ready to hear it, and the ability to enjoy the one life we get is inextricably linked to optimism, by land or by sea, by hog or by boat. In this arena, Bob has led by example, well-trusted and well-loved, among bikers and sailors alike. And I wouldn't be surprised if he and Jody go on to make another mark in a future generation of people who live in the hills. I'd be delighted to follow them there, even if it means more deadlines.

Tania Aebi
October 2005

Introduction

*I*f there is just one thing a person learns while cruising the world, it is just how little he really knew when he left. The first time I went on a long voyage, over 30 years ago, I felt as if I knew everything, and I was about to descend on the world and show them just how little they knew.

When you are young, you think you pretty much know everything. At 13 you have all life's answers. As you start to approach 30 you realize that maybe there are some things you still need to learn. Of course by the time you are 50 you know just how little true knowledge you have at your command.

As you reach the later years, you start to realize the horrible truth. We know nothing.

Cruising is pretty much the same way. As you set out on a voyage you are sure you planned for all contingencies. As the time and miles roll by, your first realization is, the problems you have planned for are not the real problems. They are unimportant. How many years you can keep canned goods has dropped to a relatively insignificant level on your list of things that are important.

If nothing else is to be learned from an extended cruise, it is that life is out there. What you have done in your lifetime to enable you to depart on an epic voyage pales by comparison to what you will find once you have untied the dock-lines and set sail.

The learning starts the day you leave the dock, and it never stops. And the funny thing is, the more you learn, the more you are aware of what you don't know.

When you meet people who have cruised extensively, if there is just one common bond, it is their ability to stay composed in just about any situation. I really don't know where this composure comes from, but you can see it as something tangible, a look in their eye, and smile on their face when they are looking back at the voyage.

Just about every world cruiser I have ever met has one thing in common. They are all either planning to get back "out there," or they are already out there, returning to do mundane things like earn the "fun tickets" needed to stay out cruising, or coming back to visit friends and relatives who haven't got the intestinal fortitude to take off on a world quest.

In the almost ten years since starting *Latitudes & Attitudes* Magazine I have tried to pass on not any special knowledge gleaned from our cruising life, but rather some of the feelings learned. As I cruised the biggest surprise to me was what became important, and what was swept away. In the editorials I wrote I found a place to pass on these lessons, and to pass on some of what I found out there.

Myself.

PART 1

The Learning Curve

It's not the place, it's the time

――――▶◀――――

*I*t was the best sunset I ever experienced. In the 13 years since, every time I see a nice sunset I always say to myself, or to whoever is in earshot, "Yeah, it's a nice one, but not as nice as the one I saw when I was crossing the equator back in '92."

Usually, unless I am stopped, I launch into the story of "the best sunset I ever saw."

Recently I was perusing some photos that I'd taken during that voyage across the Pacific, and I happened upon a picture that I'd taken of that particular sunset.

It was a great sunset, no doubt about it, but I have to admit, I have seen one or two that rivaled it, or might even have surpassed it.

So I started cranking back my cranium and trying to figure out just what the hell made me so sure that was the best sunset I had ever experienced.

It wasn't the colors. I'd seen colors as bright or as varied hundreds of times. As I looked at the photo I realized it really wasn't the sunset that had been so perfect, it had been the whole day, the state of mind, and the company I was with.

You know what I mean? It's like, have you ever gone back to a place that was home to you, and felt that it was cold and impersonal?

I know that I went to visit the place where I was brought

up, and I was extremely disillusioned. I had always thought of it as home, but the same streets, the same school and the same house just didn't feel like home any more.

And then it hit me, right between the baby blues. You can never go home. Home is a time, not a place. It's not only the surroundings, but the events and the people and even the weather and the state of the world. It all combines to create the feeling you have in your head.

When I analyze that particular sunset, it becomes obvious. I could never experience a sunset like that again.

I was about to cross the equator and I was for the very first time in control of my own vessel. After years of cruising the Northern Hemisphere, I was about to enter a whole new world. Add to that the fact that I was returning to where the sailing bug first hit me, on the island of Moorea, more than 30 years ago. That might have influenced my eyes a bit as well.

And then there was Jody. We had been friends for years, and had been going together for the past eight or nine months as we prepared the boat for our voyage, but all of a sudden it was more than that. At 48, I thought I was probably falling in love again.

Add to that the weather. For the previous few days we'd been blown south by a pretty good weather front, and all of a sudden we were drifting along on a sea of glass. The sounds of Eric Kunzel and the Cincinnati Pops Orchestra was coming over the outside speakers with an instrumental version of Chris Cross's "Sailing," and all was right with the world.

Even the events of the world were good. 9/11 was still years in the future, and O.J. was just a bad actor and not a suspected murderer. Even our political climate was pretty mundane. It all came together on that day, along with a classic sunset that, to me, would be the best ever.

The next time you have a feeling come over you, as you first set your sails, or have a first landfall, or leave on an adventurous voyage, enjoy that feeling.

Because if there is one truth, it is that you can never go home. It's not a place, it's a state of mind.

So enjoy it while you can.

Love/hate relationship

━━━━━━━━━━━►◄━━━━━━━━━━━

*T*here are days when I love my boat and the way she sails so much it almost makes Jody jealous. She says I get a look in my eye when I first catch sight of her, anchored out, when we have been ashore for a while, and she wants to know why I don't get that look when I see her.

It's at times like those that I softly remind her about the days I stomp my feet and scream at the top of my lungs, "I hate boats!"

You know those days. We all have them. When you are sitting at anchor, enjoying a sunny Sunday afternoon, your heart swelling with emotion for your vessel, and all of a sudden you notice that the bilge pump has gone off. You roll your head to the side, being ever vigilant to make sure that the water spewing from your vessel doesn't leave a slick, so the powers that be can hand you a bill for a few grand due to increased ecological pressure from the local tree huggers.

All of a sudden you see that there is, indeed, a slight sheen to the water. It's not bad, but maybe you should check it out.

And so you put down your book and head down below. It's a good day, and this shouldn't take too long, right? At least that's what you think.

As with all little problems, this one isn't quite as easily

fixed as you at first thought. When you lift the floor boards you notice that the reason it was just a slight sheen is because the bilge pump only pumped a little bit of water out. As you look for the problem you see it. Your bilge pump seems to be leaking.

But wait. How does a bilge pump leak? They are built to pump.

And so it is, a few minutes later you find yourself hanging by your knees in the bilge, with a screwdriver in one hand, and a large mallet in the other, up to your elbows in bilge-slime.

Things are still not too bad. At least they weren't. It seems that when you put the screwdriver down it rolled into the bilge, and when you whacked the bilge pump with the mallet (isn't that how you fix the damn things?) it sucked the screwdriver into the intake. What fun!

So now you are pretty much into a position that, if you saw a contortionist on TV do it, you'd think it was some kind of optical illusion.

But you have managed to get the bilge pump into your hand, and have just about got the screwdriver pulled out. That's when you hear, "Thwack!"

Now I know you have been around boats for a while, and thwack is just about the worst sound a boater can hear. Thud, thunk and ping pale in comparison to thwack.

As you turn your head just enough to catch your hair in a nearby hose clamp, you discover that the thwack was made when your mallet, which you'd laid down to get the screwdriver, dropped off the ledge, and fell three feet, right on top of your new $1,500 inverter/charger. And now it's making a new sound. It sounds as if you are frying bacon.

But it doesn't smell like bacon. It smells like burning rubber.

Burning rubber? What rubber? Where? That's what you ask yourself as you try and extract yourself from the contortionist's hell you have worked yourself into.

Once out you find that the shorted charger has overloaded the cables, shorting out your whole electrical system, and your wife is now running out of the aft head with her hair streaming a smoky trail.

It seems that just about the time the mallet hit the inverter, she turned on the hair dryer, and the full force of the short jumped to the dryer, which caught her hair on fire.

Of course you reach for the first available fire-fighting apparatus, which happens to be the bucket sitting right next to you, and you douse her with it. Only trying to help, of course.

How were you supposed to remember you'd just filled it from the bilge, and it was full of bilge slime? Hey, you were just trying to help!

It's at about this point when you are wondering just what the hell it was that made you think you actually enjoyed your boat. In fact, if you weren't so busy wiping the grease off your wife and the cabin sole, you'd probably be standing on deck jumping up and down screaming, "I Hate Boats!"

A couple hours later, after you and your wife have downed a few Valium and a Xanax and she has returned to being a human being (who was the creature she'd turned into anyway?), you've replaced the bilge pump and inverter/charger. Once again you are sitting on deck, living large and loving life.

Sitting back at times like that, I realize that having a boat is a true love/hate relationship.

They say the opposite of love isn't hate, it's apathy. I don't know anyone who's apathetic about their boat. Do you?

Preparation, perspiration and luck

After five or six extended cruises I learned a little trick. When I plan a long voyage I always leave a little "catch up" time somewhere in the plan.

For example, if I plan a trip down through the Caribbean from, let's say, Fort Lauderdale, I will make a plan to be out of the hurricane area before said windy things start blowing. That means either south to the Grenada, Trinidad, Venezuela area, or north to either the East Coast of the U.S. or the Azores, heading to the Med.

When I make my plans I've learned to leave a little playtime in the schedule. I guess there are folks out there who don't set a plan. They just sail down there, hang around playing until just before it's time to get out, and then they hightail it. I prefer to know where I will end up, but I don't want to schedule myself into oblivion. Thus the free time.

One year we were heading back from the Med and ended up in Antigua. We figured we had plenty of time to play, as I had left my extra month in the plan. Then my generator decided it was too tired to run anymore. Two weeks of my extra month went to cruising the Antigua and Barbuda area waiting for my genset to be rebuilt.

When it was done we started our leisurely cruise down through the Leeward and Windward Islands, when the rebuilt genset decided it wasn't happy about the rebuild and it died again. This time we were sitting in the anchorage in Bequia, which is one of our favorite places to hang out.

So we did. Hang out that is. Two weeks until the genset was ready again, and we were exiting the Leewards right on time.

But it isn't always broken parts that slow you down. Many times it is when you find a very special place, and you just don't want to leave.

This happened to us in French Polynesia. You are pretty restricted by the storm season when you cruise there if, like me, you believe in the safety of seasonal travel. We sailed across the equator in mid-May, arriving in the Marquesas at the start of cruising season.

We spent a few weeks in the Marquesas and then sailed through the Tuamotus, arriving in the Society Islands with our extra month still intact. When we got to Raiatea, Bora Bora, Tahaa and Huahine, we fell in love with the place. We spent an extra three weeks there, and it couldn't have been better.

But we still had one extra week in our pocket. As we sailed toward the Northern Cook Islands and our target stop of Suverov Island, a storm blew in. We tucked in out of the bad weather into an island we had never even heard of, much less planned on visiting—the little pinprick on your chart called Mopelia.

Probably one of the most memorable stops I can think of in my life of cruising was that extra week we spent lying around after the storm blew by on an island that, if we hadn't set aside that time, we never would have known.

Now I know that there are a bunch of you out there wondering why I set a schedule in the first place. Most folks picture cruising as wandering around from port to port, with no real idea of where you are going or when. I did that the first decade or so that I cruised. I would say something like "I'm gonna go cruise Mexico!" and I'd be off.

Three months later I'd be bored silly sitting at anchor, wondering where to go next. I didn't have any plans. I didn't think about laying out a voyage. I didn't need to. I was a cruiser, damn it! And cruisers don't need to make no stinking plans.

Years later I realized how much more I enjoyed cruising with a plan in mind. I'd spent my life living on a schedule. I didn't know it then, but I liked being on a schedule. I liked planning a voyage as much as I did going on it. Maybe more! In my plans everything went perfect! How kewl is that!

The extra time I always include in my plan allows for a little deviation from what I plan. If I don't have a breakdown, and I don't find a surprise area, it's okay. I just carry over my extra time to the next section of the voyage.

A successful voyage is 50% preparation, 40% perspiration and 10% luck!

Rules . . . we don't need no rules!

W hy is it they always give the worst winds the cutest names? We discovered this phenomenon as we were heading south to the Panama Canal on our way to Europe back in 1994.

Having crossed the Sea of Tehuantepec numerous times, I was well aware of the dreaded Tehuantepecer—a funny name with a deadly twist. The Tehuantepecer comes out of nowhere, with winds gusting upwards of 100 mph! Not something to be trifled with. So, being a careful skipper, I dutifully monitored Herb on Southbound II's weather watch, and we planned our crossing when we had at least a 24-hour hole.

Having crossed this area a few times, I was becoming complacent.

Rule #1: Never become complacent!

As we had a good opening, I decided to head out. Normally I would "keep one foot on the beach," which is the normal practice for this area. That way, if the wind does come up there is no fetch, as the wind always comes off the land. 100 mph winds are not too bad if there are no seas with them.

I talked with a large powerboat I saw on the horizon. It seems they were heading straight out across the sea. I asked why, and they said the weather service they subscribed to gave them a three-day opening.

After some thought I figured, what the heck, let's go for it!

Rule #2: Never figure "What the heck."

So three days later, our powerboat buddies are tucked into Bahia Cocoa sipping tropical drinks and enjoying the balmy breezes, while the LOST SOUL chugged along on diesel power, as there was no wind at all.

Just before dawn on our last day, we started to get a little wind.

Our loud-mouthed captain (that'd be me!) piped up with "Okay, we got a little wind, let's see if we can't get a little more!"

Rule #3: Never ask for more wind!

You see, I figured we were far enough away from the peninsula where the dreaded Tehuantepecer was born, so a little wind would be nice.

Yes, a little wind would have been nice.

Anyone out there ever seen all the boats that are named Papagallo? You have any idea where the cute name comes from? After all, it is such a great name; Papagallo. It flows, right?

Well, a little after dawn the crew of the LOST SOUL started to become acquainted with the word Papagallo a little more intimately than we would have wished for.

By noon we had about 50 knots of wind blowing right on our nose. It seems that a less publicized occurrence for the area was none other than the cutely titled phenomenon for which all these cute little sailboats were named—the Papagallo storm.

This differs from the Tehuantepecer in that it does not blow out of the north across the Mexican peninsula, but it prefers to blow from the southeast, across Nicaragua. Actually a little out of the ESE, just about where you wouldn't want wind to come from if you were sailing to, say, Costa Rica. Which we were.

Rule #4: When cruising, there is either too much wind or not enough, but it's always on the nose!

As the day progressed we rode a dual-edged sword. On the one hand, every hour saw the wind increase, along with the seas. On the other hand, we also got closer to land, which reduced the fetch, so the seas were not as bad as they could have been.

Around 3 p.m. we were within sight of land, and a welcome sight it was. Just before dark we pulled in behind a cliff and dropped anchor.

We sat there for the night and about half the next day while the Papagallo blew. Whitecaps whirled behind us as the wind dropped from the cliff to scour the sea.

And then I noticed that there weren't as many whitecaps about a mile or so south. After assuring myself that it was not, indeed, a mirage, we hoisted anchor and headed in that direction.

Every few hundred feet found the wind dwindling. About a mile away it was actually warm! But behind us the winds still howled.

We were soon anchored in a cute little bay with clear blue water and no wind at all.

Looking back at the windline, we were soon lulled back into cruising mode. We felt more than a little pride in having experienced a Papagallo so intimately.

Rule #5: An ordeal becomes an adventure after the passage of enough time.

Too safe?

————————————⟶◂————————————

When we set sail for the open seas, one of the things that seems to weigh the heaviest on a cruiser's mind is the fact that we leave the security of a known for the insecurity of an unknown.

Oh, you can put this into a lot of different contexts, but in the end, that is one fear that has cancelled more voyages than any other—fear of the unknown.

What about storms? What about pirates? What if my boat springs a leak? What if I run out of rum? The fact that any of us ever go out there seems remarkable to a vast majority of people. They not only would never sail a boat across an ocean, but they think we're nuts sailing out of the sight of land. They would never do that. It's a silly thing to do!

I recall being in an anchorage in La Cruz, Venezuela; actually it was at the CMO Boatyard. We'd hauled out to get the hull painted, as we had sailed about 50,000 miles in the previous four years, and we had put a few dings, dents and scrapes in the hull.

While we were in the yard, some of the local boating community told us we shouldn't go into La Cruz, which was about a $2 cab fare away and the main town in the area. Their reasoning was, about a month and a half earlier a couple of boaters had been mugged and robbed. They were accosted, their purse and wallet stolen from them, and they were knocked to the pavement.

•••

Because of this, the 40-50 people who were living in the marina area had avoided going to town. They, of course, didn't want to get mugged.

Who would, right?

Well, after the good-intentioned contingent from this group of cruisers finished telling us it wasn't safe in town, Jody and I sat there and finished our beers, and then walked out of the boat yard and started looking for a cab. We couldn't wait to get to town!

These people were remaining captives in their safe marina because one couple had been mugged over a month earlier! In the meantime, in Los Angeles the previous evening, approximately three people had been murdered, at least a dozen shot, and there were so many robberies and muggings they wouldn't even appear in the newspapers! And I've lived there most of my life!

I felt like I could walk through that town with a couple hundred dollar bills hanging out of my pocket and be a heck of a lot safer than I would ever be in a safe place like, say, New York, Detroit, Miami or even Prescott, Arizona!

This same scenario once almost kept us from visiting one of the best places we stayed while we were cruising the world. When we planned our voyage to the Med, Jody and I had pretty much written off the mainland of Italy. We had been told by cruisers that if you anchored in places like Naples, you had to keep a guard at night because they would steal stuff off your boat.

Because of this, we decided to visit Corsica and Sardinia, and then bypass Naples. Due to a breakdown, we had to adjust those plans, and we were forced to go to Naples to await a part. We ended up staying 10 days in a suburb of

Naples, the town of Baia, and we fell in love with the place. The people were great, and we didn't hear of a single incident of theft while we were there.

As cruisers, we have to keep things in perspective; balance reality in a number of ways. Yes, if you walk through a crowd in the Naples airport, I would suggest keeping a hand on your wallet. When I walk through LAX or Kennedy, I do the same. That's not paranoia, that's using your common sense. But not going to the airport at all?

Okay, got your PFD on? Got your tether hooked up? Don't leave the harbor . . . the water's pretty deep out there.

Yeah, right!!

Let's just go sailing!

Nautical history, who needs it?

><──

I can vividly recall almost 30 years ago, the feeling I had the first time I was on a sailboat and felt the mainsail set and fill with wind. I was about 28 years old (yeah, I am that old!), and I remember how I grabbed onto the shiny chrome thing next to me (that'd be a cleat), and felt my knuckles go white as the boat started to flip over, or at least that's what I thought it was doing.

I had just made an offer on this Cal 28 named ROGUE. The only reason I was buying it was: a) I had just made some money and it was burning a hole in my pocket; b) my business partner called that morning from Tahiti saying he'd just met some guys and they asked him to join them on a sail from Moorea to Hawaii, and; c) I'd made the mistake of going to Capt. Ahab's Coffee Shop at the marina for lunch, and saw the guy sticking a for sale sign on the boat.

So anyway, here I was, hanging onto a protruding piece of chromed bronze as I was about to end my life on my very first sail. Of this I was sure. Then the seller screamed at me from the wheel, "Hey, grab the sheet and ease her a little."

I was trying to figure out why in the world he'd want to be messing with sheets, when he let go of the wheel and somehow actually managed to walk across the vertical (or so it seemed to me) cockpit to a rope hanging from a thinga-mabob that held it clamped firmly in place. He miraculously let out some rope, and the boat returned to an almost livable angle of tilt.

I watched in total awe as this otherwise normal looking person turned the boat around by doing a bunch of magical stuff with ropes and a stick he kept pushing back and forth (that'd be the tiller). Soon, I started to release the death grip I had on the doodad.

We sailed for about an hour, and when it was time to turn the boat back to the harbor I actually was able to help. Well, okay, I was actually able to get out of the way. But that was a start.

I made a deal with the guy to teach me to sail if I bought the boat. He was leaving for Hawaii in five days on a 50-foot steel ketch, so I talked him into three lessons. Anyone can learn to sail in three lessons, right?

By the end of day three I was actually able to back the boat out of the slip, get it out of the channel without hitting more than one or two protruding objects, and pull the rope that made the mainsail go up.

In his defense, he did try to teach me the names of some of the ropes, but I thought that was all kinda silly. A rope is a rope. Halyard, sheet, topping lift, who really uses words like that anyway? A rope is a rope.

I must digress here for a moment. You see, at this time in my life I was publisher of a motorcycle magazine. My life consisted of riding around the country on a bike and getting stories. Sailing seemed like a whole other world to me. On a bike, a wheel is a wheel, and a bolt is a bolt. Rope should be rope.

For the next three months, every afternoon about 2 p.m. I would grab my editor who went by the unlikely name of

Degenerate Jim, and head to the harbor. We would park our bikes in the lot, walk down the docks in our boots and Levis, untie the docklines and head out of the harbor. By the end of month three I had reached the most dangerous time of being a sailor—when you think you know everything.

By now, my partner had returned from sailing the Pacific and told me he'd met a guy with a big topsail schooner who wanted to sail to Central America. Was I interested in going? It took about five seconds to figure out how to arrange it, and I was signed on.

It took about a month for the STONE WITCH to provision and sail south from San Francisco to Redondo Beach. In that time, I sailed every day. A week before the STONE WITCH came in, I sold ROGUE to a friend of mine and was ready.

After a farewell party that won't soon be forgotten in our harbor, we departed. As we cleared the harbor Captain Olsen screamed to hoist the rode. I stared at him blankly. What's a rode?

He then started speaking in tongues or something. Hoist the halyard, tighten the sheet, set the stays'l halyard, ease the topping lift.

All of a sudden it started to sink into my alleged mind. Yes, there really is a reason for all of the nomenclature of a boat, and there is a history behind every name.

Life cycles

———————▶◀———————

*J*ody and I decided to anchor in a very small and tucked away bay on the island of Tahaa in the Society Islands of French Polynesia. For the previous two months we'd had visitors who'd flown in to sail with us, and all of a sudden we found ourselves, just the two of us, with nothing to do in paradise.

In the morning we took the dinghy ashore tying up to a small wooden pier on the shore. We wandered about a quarter mile up the gravel road to where we found a small store. They didn't speak English, and we didn't speak French, but there was no communication problem. They smiled, we smiled, and we walked through their small store. They didn't have much to offer. Just some basics. However, on the counter there was a plate filled with fresh homemade sugar donuts.

We grabbed a couple and wandered leisurely back to the LOST SOUL. I remember kicking back there on the foredeck of the boat. The sun was just starting to get warm and we were surrounded by lush tropical growth on the shore, as we munched on those great sugar donuts.

I couldn't even remember what "real life" was like. We sat there talking about what people back home might be doing, trying to remember what it had been like. I remember thinking how it all seemed as if our past life had been a bad dream, a nightmare.

How could people live like that, we wondered? Why would they?

Many months later, when we returned from that voyage, we stopped to visit our friends and families. We told stories of our adventures, and had countless slide parties where we would recount the adventures and the misadventures.

As time rolled on the ordeals turned into adventures. The knockdown in the Alenuihaha Channel went from being a frightening experience to being one of the highlights of our voyage. As more time passed even fixing a broken head took on magical properties. The storms that seemed to roll on for days now dwindled in our memories to a mere wisp of wind that lasted only an hour or two. The fear of our first time hitting bottom now became a point of pride. We'd always chime in with, "There are only two types of sailors; those who have gone aground and those who are going to!"

We took off again, and sailed to the other end of the earth. We visited ancient civilizations, met paupers and princes, dined in great restaurants and at tavernas in harbors that have been in use longer than mankind can remember.

And that voyage too came to an end. After years we returned to our home base, and once again the slide shows started, and once again, in the telling, ordeals became great adventures. Selective memory is a wondrous thing, and before long all we could remember was the dream life we had lived for so many years. A dream, that's what it all seemed.

I can still remember the taste of that sugar donut on Tahaa. I can still feel the grains of sugar caught in my beard, and remember with total clarity the way Jody's hair gleamed in the surreal light of a tropical paradise, but it does seem more a dream.

And therein lies the truth of the matter. When you are out there doing it; living and loving life, you think back on your pre-cruising existence, it all seems just a terrible nightmare. On the other hand, when you return to reality, what was out there seems more like it was a dream.

So the question arises, why would anyone in their right mind want to live a nightmare? And the next logical progression of this quandary is, why am I sitting here in a nightmare writing about dreaming?

As this is our fifth anniversary issue it seems like this is the time to get out there and live the dream again. As of this issue I have found an investor, who has agreed to hand over quantities of fun tickets and to take over the day-to-day operation of *Latitudes & Attitudes*. I have assured him how much fun it is to deal with printers, distribution folk and subscription fulfillment.

I then convinced him that the best way for me to handle the arduous task of being managing editor would be to make the ultimate sacrifice, and to actually go out there on the ocean, on a boat, and send in the latest news from the very source.

Ahhh, the sacrifices Jody and I are about to make!!

Now, let me see, where were those sugar donuts?

The crew of the UNICORN

➤◄

S ailing aboard the tall ship UNICORN on a recent voyage to the Dry Tortugas, I sat enthralled as I watched the crew go about their duties. It was an eye-opener.

The UNICORN is a true working square-rigged topsail schooner and there are no winches on the boat, so when you want to tighten a sail, you manually jerk on the lines to do so. Working on this boat, you feel like you are pushing it across the ocean, and take pride in that fact.

Watching the crew work the boat brought back a flood of feelings from 30 years ago, when I first sailed on a similar ship, and learned the true feeling of the sea, being a part of a crew.

The whole crew worked great as a team, and each one of them brought their own personality into the group. That's what makes a ship's company what it is, the combination of personalities.

Watching 22-year-old Emma go from one area to another, with nary a word, just knowing what had to be done and doing the job, was like watching poetry in motion. The look of concentration on her face, or of pure effort as she'd tug on a line, made you respect her and all of a sudden her tender years were forgotten. She's a skilled sailor doing every bit the job that sailors have done for the past 500 years, and she has earned the respect of her crewmates as well as mine.

And then there's Patrick, who would scamper up the ratlines to the topsail at a moment's notice. Another act of poetry in motion. Poetry. That's what the whole crew created as they worked together.

If there is no other reason for a sailor to board a tall ship and set sail, it has to be to see just how well a good crew can come together to create a team. It took me years, but it finally sunk in. That's why they call these ship's "training vessels."

Most of you are aware that tall ships, for the most part, belong to ASTA—the American Sail Training Association. I often wondered if there were truly that many people who needed sail training. Now I realize that they don't just teach how to sail. They teach how to live and work as a team.

Watching the skipper, Captain Scott, as he'd handle the boat and the crew, was like watching a maestro working with a well-rehearsed orchestra. With a nod and a word, often shouted to get it from the stern to the foredeck, the crew seemed to know or even guess the next step.

Scott's bride-to-be, Taylor, had just signed on for this voyage, but she had sailed as crew before, and when there was a line to be tugged, or a fender that needed to be placed, she was right there, digging in and doing her part.

Julian has been sailing on tall ships since he was 13 years old. At 19 he has a presence and bearing that belie his tender age. He uses his 6'7" frame to bear the load when other crewmen need some real beef. Unlike most teenagers, he doesn't shirk his duties, and in fact he seems to seek out the toughest jobs and attack them with a relish that would make any parent, not to mention skipper or crewmate, proud.

And then there's Sara, quiet and timid Sara. Watching her when she is working is watching pure concentration. She actually would seek out the hardest or dirtiest job on the boat, and take an obvious pride in how she would attack each problem. The windlass a little rusty? No problem, she would be the first one with a wire brush, solvent and paint, and soon it looked like new. Ship's flag falling apart? She got the sewing kit at hand, and soon it flew high on the mast.

I think that I finally understand what ASTA, and sailing in general, are all about. It's not about teaching or learning how to set a sail, or how to drop an anchor, or even how to navigate a treacherous pass. What you learn is what most of our young people are lacking more than the basic three r's. You learn pride in a job well done, and self worth.

That's what a life at sea can teach us all. Working a tall ship, or sailing a 22 footer around the bay, requires self-reliance, self-assurance and an ability to handle yourself.

When two people are on the same boat, they are crew. They are no longer two individuals, but a team, and every teammate has his or her specific job. And these jobs are much better accomplished when all hands work together.

The feeling of arriving at anchor after working a ship on a voyage, hoisting a cold one in salute to a job well done, is priceless.

The best anchor ever made

So the other day I'm sitting and downing a cold one with my father-in-law, who built his own boat some 20 years ago and has been cruising the Caribbean ever since. The conversation came around to anchors, and all of a sudden he turned into a preacher. As far as he was concerned there was only one anchor. A Delta.

Someone else at the table smiled knowingly, and espoused the virtues of his favorite anchor, the Fortress. As far as he was concerned, it was the only anchor that actually worked.

An old salt sitting at the next table cut in to say that he has been using a Fisherman for over 40 years, and there was none that could compare.

What skipper on earth has never uttered the phrase "I use a (blank), and it's the best anchor there is!"? Come on. Fess up. All sailors are loyal to the hunk of iron hanging off the front of their boat. Of course they are. If they didn't think it best they wouldn't have it hanging there.

And rest assured, all of these same folks are also guilty of muttering something like "G%$#$@!! D*&^%$!! F&*^%$$## hunk of iron couldn't hold a donut in a cup of coffee!" too.

It's actually a lot of fun, when sitting around the old palapa table, wriggling your toes in the sand on a warm day ashore, tipping a few of the local brew while discussing voyages, to throw in a little bit of a challenge. You know, something like this:

"You know, the best anchor ever made is the (insert your anchor here)!"

A second will tick by, and then it will start. At first it will be cordial.

"Yeah, that's a good one, but the Hunk-O-Iron 3206 has held me in every blow I've ever been in. Why, I remember back in the summer of '86 when . . ." and the stories about anchors holding will then commence.

After each skipper at the table has sworn to the validity of having their particular hunk of rusted iron, then it's time to get to the real truth. It's here you introduce what I like to call the "rub." All good conversations need a little friction, right?

"You know, my Hunk-O-Iron 3206 is great, but . . ." and then you go into one particular time when your hunk of iron let you down. Now the stories going around the table will change.

"Ya know, yer right! When I was trying to drop a hook off of Aruba in '93 . . ."

Sit back now, and listen as each person trashes their unsinkable anchor.

I have found that, with three or four skippers at a sitting, one can, with the correct injection, stretch a cold one into a complete afternoon and evening meal of entertainment and fun, just by using this technique.

And what's even more fun is when you spark up the stories with "and then I read this story in Boat Anchoring Annual, and they said. . . ."

Because, as we all know, anyone who gets their by-line

in a boating magazine is an instant authority. Just ask me, I know. I usta couln't even spell editer, and now I is one!

I have dropped hooks in probably every kind of bottom and weather you can imagine. During our last little 50,000-mile, five-year jaunt, we figured we were actually tied to a dock or in a slip less than 90 days in those five years. Say we were under sail crossing oceans seven times, at about two-three weeks each, so there's another 150 days. That leaves about 1,500 days at anchor.

And I don't know a damn thing about anchoring. Nada! Zilch!

People ask me at seminars about it, and I gotta fess up. I'm about as ignorant about anchoring as the first day I puked over the side of my first boat.

What do I carry on my boat? All the iron I can find, beg, borrow or steal, that's what. At the present time I have a 110-pound Bruce hanging off the port bow, a 65-pound stainless plow on the starboard, a very old 65-pound CQR as a backup below decks, to use as a second anchor in-line if needed in a strong blow.

On the aft rail I have a 65-pound high-tensile Danforth, strapped next to a 66-pound Bruce. Below I usually keep a 95-pound Fisherman, just in case.

Any one of these anchors has held well in perfect weather and bottom conditions. I can also tell you, with as much honesty, that there are times when each of these would not hold.

If there is any little wisdom that I can pass on without fear of being contradicted, it is this. Always get an anchor at least one size larger than they say you should, and always lay out more chain or rode than is suggested by the experts. You won't be sorry.

Okay. Time to hoist that rusting hunk of iron, and do what boats are supposed to do. Go sailing.

Regulations

———————————➤◄———————————

Why can't the damn bureaucraps leave us alone?
Here we are enjoying a lifestyle that hurts no
one, and faster than an alligator can run through a handbag
factory, the dunderheads in government decide we should
be regulated. After all, we might hurt ourselves out there,
right?

So, due to our inadequacy and mental dysfunction
(after all, we were crazy enough to leave all our stuff behind, and move onto a boat!) they feel they must legislate
for our protection.

So what has gotten my panties in a wad, you ask? Well,
it's a small article I wrote about last issue here in the rag. It
said some idiot was trying to legislate that all boaters must
wear PFDs (Personal Flotation Devices) while on their
boats.

Uh, excuse me. Got a sec? Can we discuss sleeping
arrangements here? What happens if me and Jody are get-
tin' frisky in the aft cabin, and along comes the harbor patrol and arrests us. No, not for illegal use of a feather duster,
but for not having our life vests on.

I can see us now, standing before Judge Judy. The pros-
ecutor has a handful of 8x10 color glossy photos, complete
with arrows and captions on the back, taken through our aft
windows.

Far fetched? Ain't gonna happen? Well, you gotta keep

in mind that the average Joe out there doesn't know anything about boats. If it's put up for a vote, the majority of people in the US would probably say "Kewl. Why should those people be happy and carefree? Let them wear a PFD, it's safer."

Yeah, we know it couldn't happen any more than some idiot passing a law that seat belts should be worn by all drivers, including motorcyclists. Oops, I forgot. They did that one.

A couple of decades ago we thought boaters would always have a place to drop a hook while cruising the coastline and not have to pay for the privilege. Now finding a free anchorage is like winning the lottery. Some do, but not me.

And why has this happened? Because we, the folks who use them, are a minority, so we don't make the rules. Anyone who doesn't have a boat will vote to charge mega-bucks for anchoring. Why should all them "rich yachties" be able to anchor for free? Make 'em pay!

The fact that it just flat doesn't make sense to charge someone to drop a hook in the ocean has nothing to do with it. This is a democracy, and the majority rules. Unfortunately the majority don't own boats. Ergo the laws that are passed reflect that.

So what else are the bureaucraps likely to foist on us? Well, let's see. They might pull the main focus of the Coast Guard from safety at sea to drug intervention. Oh yeah, they did that already. Almost forgot.

Well, maybe they could come up with something really idiotic. Hey, I got it! How about every time a boat enters a harbor we have someone come aboard and put a poisonous die tablet in their head, so they don't pee in the ocean?

Yeah, let's do that. Who cares what it does to the waters when it is discharged; can't have people pee in the ocean, right?

And maybe we can charge a special tax for people who are silly enough to buy boats! Yeah, that's a good one. But wait, they did that, and people went to other countries to buy their boats, and it almost killed the boating industry in the US. Oh well, they're just boaties, so it don't matter.

But I gotta tell ya. It's still great. Even if they do want to regulate the fun out of it. They just can't do it. You know why?

Because we can always go away! If they start screwing with me where I am, I can just untie the lines. It's my choice.

When I started cruising I wanted to make my crossings as short as possible. Two weeks at sea was what we had to do to get to where we wanted to go. Now, some twenty years later, I find I prefer the long crossings. Days at sea are pure heaven. I am responsible for my own actions. If I am stupid enough to dump my head and then go swimming in the discharge, shame on me. I'll learn. But I don't need some idiot who has never set foot on a boat to tell me.

You do start to get a little gun shy after cruising in regulated waters, and you can start to forget to beauty of the lifestyle.

I remember when we pulled into Suverov Island in the Northern Cook islands, after three months in French Polynesia. We dropped our hook in the lagoon, and as I watched it set I saw a man get into his small boat and start rowing out to see us. My first reaction was, "Oh no. It's starting!"

and I asked Jody to go below and get our papers, passports and ships documents.

As he pulled up beside the boat he asked "Hey, we have bar-b-q on the beach tonight at sunset. You come?"

There are some local regulations we can live with, ya know?

Un-civilized?

———————►◄———————

I really didn't know what to think. After we entered the harbor at Fatu Hiva in the Marquesas, we pulled in as close as we could to shore and set our hook in about 30 feet of crystal clear water. The harbor was surrounded by lush green hills and over a dozen colorful outriggers were anchored in the bay.

We'd timed our arrival well; the sun was just setting as the snubber line was attached to the chain, and we sat back with a cold one to celebrate another great day of sailing in the South Pacific.

All of a sudden we heard some voices, and two outriggers were pulling alongside the LOST SOUL. My first thought was to reach for the machete I keep by the nav-station as it was closer than the shotgun buried in the aft cabin. Just before my hand closed on the haft of the long, cold blade I saw a smiling face looking over the rail.

Six young men filled the two canoes. They were all large, and covered with tattoos. My first thought? We were about to meet our first real-life pirates. This was from years of conditioning in a civilization that has bred violence as an artform. But then it hit me. I'm not in civilization any more! This is Polynesia, and tattoos don't indicate anti-social behavior, but are a sign of stature in the community.

Kewl! I'm covered with 'em!

Soon the six would-be attackers were sitting around

the aft deck, singing some of the local songs and accompanying the songs with the ukeleles they'd brought and a guitar we had on board. They had rowed out to welcome us to their island. A Polynesian custom older than anyone can remember.

We listened, laughed and even sang them a few songs from our home island. You know, some Buffett and Beatles stuff. Even though none of them spoke a word of English, and none of us a word of Polynesian or French, we spent two hours getting acquainted.

As they sang I broke out my video camera and filmed the intercourse between our crew and theirs. The songs, the smiles and the hand signals were almost comical.

In fact, it was so comical I figured they might like to see the video. After they'd finished their songs we indicated they should come below, to see the video on the TV.

Once below they gazed around the LOST SOUL in wonder. I flipped on the TV and plugged the video recorder into it. In a couple of seconds their singing filled the air, and there they were in living color.

They sat there as if spellbound. Then one of them recognized his friend on the screen, and he started to giggle. They talked excitedly between themselves, and couldn't stop giggling.

It seems this was the first time they had ever seen a television set. The fact that they were starring in the video didn't even hit them until after the first few seconds of being shocked at seeing full color moving photos with sound.

It hadn't even dawned on me that these guys had never seen a television.

In the next few days we were greeted each morning by two or three of our new friends, and they would take us to find particularly good fruits and vegetables growing on the island, and one day they led us to a beautiful waterfall in a small valley a couple miles from where we anchored.

In the ensuing months, which turned into years, we would meet other people we would get to know, in spite of the language barriers. But none had such an impact as the first meeting, there in Fatu-Hiva, where I first realized that the most civilized people on earth are those we tend to call uncivilized.

Sailors are weird

>———◄

*T*hey say that variety is the spice of life. Of course we have no idea who the heck "they" are, but that doesn't matter. They said it, and that's that. I'm not one to argue with them. Of course not. Hell, they may be bigger than I am. So, in order to avoid conflict with a much larger and more ferocious being than I, it was decided that I would take their word for it. I wanted variety. I wanted spice.

So there we were. Jody and I, and our trusty vessel The LOST SOUL. We'd been out cruising for about a year or so, and had made our way into and out of some of the most written about and photographed islands of the world. For the past year we'd been hanging out in French Polynesia, the Northern Cooks, Samoa and Tonga. They were all they were cracked up to be, and maybe a little more.

But we needed a little variety. A little spice in our lives. Being truly twisted individuals, we spun the globe we have in our main saloon, and stuck a finger into it to stop it.

And thus was born our little jaunt to get some souvlaki. Yup, the finger hit Greece. Because of this little game we played, we had all of a sudden gone from lackadaisical hang-around boat-bums, to cruisers on a mission. We had plans to make. All of a sudden life was good and full.

Now don't get me wrong. Hanging around in paradise has its advantages. I'd have to be pretty damned jaded to think it didn't. But after a couple of years, carefree drifting starts to resemble what I call aimless wandering.

Okay, so now half the cruisers in the world are about to descend on me with belaying pins held high.

You trying to make cruising look bad?

Nope. That's not it. The truth of the matter is, after I've been out for a while sailing in one area, I start to get bored.

Yeah, I know, thousands of people would give their eye-teeth to live that lifestyle. You know, for years I liked pissing people off, just by telling them the way I lived. It was almost as much fun as the lifestyle itself!

I remember when Jody and I sailed back to our home-port in the Portofino Marina, Redondo Beach, California, after cruising Hawaii and the South Pacific. Why? Well, in reality it was just to see the look in our friends' eyes when we told them; no, we weren't going to stay. We'd just sailed in to say "Hi" and were on our way to the Med.

Talk about numerous shades of green! Envy was dripping off them, like oil from an old Harley, and we loved it.

Guess that's not something one should admit to, but what the heck. I never was one to mislabel stuff. It was worth the 2,700-mile sail to come home and turn our friends green. It was great.

But that wasn't the only reason we did it. There was a need for change. We'd been cruising without a goal for a while, and all of a sudden I got excited again. Hey! A trip to plan!

I needed new charts. Bitchin! I love charts. I love the way they smell when you first roll them out.

And the thrill of finding just the right cruising guide.

How can anything compare with that? It's like a first date, one you got lucky on.

And then you get to live the adventure before you ever pull out of port. You get to go over the trip, step by step, area by area, country by country. You have to plan for the seasons, the best times to make crossings, where to provision.

Ah, it's pure paradise. Your mind lives the adventure a hundred times before you ever even cast off a line.

I can recall how excited we all got as we decided that Greece would be our destination. All the cruising guides were pulled out and the charts of Greece spread out on the saloon table. Then we all sat around, like a bunch of demented children, pointing at places that looked interesting, and where we wanted to go for sure.

The fact that we were anchored in paradise was all of a sudden forgotten. The brilliant white beach laying just a hundred yards across the crystal blue/white water of an almost uninhabited lagoon in the South Pacific was no longer of interest. We'd been there, done that, got the shirt.

And you know what, a couple of years later, as we were leaving the Med, after sailing the places we'd dreamed of and planned on, it was just as exciting planning to go back to the South Pacific, to see the people we'd met while there, and to see the places we'd missed.

Hard-fought victory

*I*t was the eleventh day of an eight-day crossing. We'd left Pago Pago on a beautiful sunny day, with 15 knots of wind and almost glassy seas. It looked to be a perfect departure.

By the afternoon the winds had shifted around. Any guesses to which direction? You got it. Right outta where we wanted to go. Lovely!

As the hours progressed into days the winds' velocity changed. Once again, class, wanna guess? Yup, you got it again. They were inching up on 35 knots, right on our nose.

On the fourth day we noticed our GPS was starting to go off. It had to be. We were making seven knots headway by sailing about 33 degrees off the winds (and off our course). But the silly electrical doodad was saying we were only doing about three knots. Silly gadget. Never did trust 'em.

But the next day, on our noon-sight, it was confirmed. We had made just 85 miles in the past 24 hours. That meant we were deep into the equatorial countercurrent.

So let's see. We have 35-knot headwinds, the seas are up to eight to 10 feet, the currents are on our nose, and we are barely able to make three knots, in the wrong direction.

Are we having fun yet? Is there anything else that can go wrong?

Never ask that question, because you don't want know the answer. In our case, the answer was a ripped main. What fun.

We get to play sew-the-sail while we drift backwards at a rate of over six knots (four knots of current and two knots of drift!).

So we decide discretion is the better part of valor, and fire up the iron genny. She sparks to life, we slam it into forward and get on course again, beating into what can only be described as a very wet purgatory.

Okay, so let's continue our little quiz. Any ideas on what happened next? Aw, always the same hands are up.

But you got it right, the engine decided it wanted a little more fuel than could be pushed through our clogged fuel filters (from all the pounding we'd done) and took the rest of the day off.

On the eleventh day we spotted Christmas Island, the first of the Line Islands. It was still one of those "you can't get there from here" sort of deals, being that it was still up-wind and up-current, but we saw the tips of the 65-foot palm trees. We knew that before sunset we would be anchored in the lee, in calm seas and enjoying a respite from the 11 days of hell.

As I dropped the hook in the crystal blue water, and watched it set 30 feet below in a cloud of coral dust, I realized how much I love cruising.

I can't think of another lifestyle that allows a person to feel the exhilaration and thrill of conquering the elements. The feeling of self-reliance that you have after battling against the winds and seas just cannot be explained to a landslug.

I remember, barely, a crossing I once made to Hawaii, in which I had what some would call a perfect crossing. You know, 20 knots of wind just slightly off your stern, with sunny skies and balmy days. It was as perfect a crossing could be. I say I barely remember it, because it has almost completely faded from my memory.

What jumps to mind is the Pago Pago to Christmas Island fiasco, or the time we blew our tranny coming out of Palmyra, and sailed 1,000 miles without a motor, through the doldrums. I can't remember the good sails, but can pull up with vivid clarity the ones that tested my soul.

I am probably a little (lot?) sick in the head, but one of the things that makes a cruise memorable for me is overcoming the obstacles. To feel that little thrill when a busted spreader is mickey-moused to get you in without losing your mast, or when you push your boat into a harbor with your dinghy because your engine died.

When sitting on a distant shore with other cruisers, downing a cold local brew, the talk always turns to, "and then the Vigero really hit the ol' mixmaster when . . .", and the stories that flow forth are always of the trials and tribulations, and never the less memorable, perfect cruises.

The next time you are being slammed by the sea gods like a red-headed step-child, take a second to think about how the story is going to sound a year later, while sitting at a dockside tavern in Greece. Think of the hours of spellbinding stories you will be able to tell your grandkids about how you overcame untold obstacles. It makes all of the strife come into perspective.

More than one old and wise guru have stated that the hard-fought victory is the one that is most thoroughly enjoyed. By putting ourselves in harm's way, by battling the same sea gods that Ulysses and Captain Cook, and a million other adventurers before us have conquered, makes it all a worthy lifestyle.

Thanks, Captain Olsen

➤◄

I was standing on the deck of the STONE WITCH, a 70-foot square-rigged topsail schooner out of San Francisco. We were headed south to Central America. It's like it was yesterday. I remember there were a couple of albatross gliding across the ocean's wave tops, and I wondered just how they managed to tip the top of the waves, without ever actually touching them.

We hoisted anchor in Redondo Beach about three days earlier, and had been underway ever since. In spite of the time we'd been out, we had only managed to cover about 55 miles. The wind gods had decided against us, and we sat rocking back and forth for the first two days, still in sight of the port.

You see, the boat didn't have an engine. It had four 21-foot oars that could be jimmied between the shrouds, and with two people on each one you could actually move the 54-ton vessel.

But not fast. No, not fast at all. So we sat.

Since we had no engine, we were pretty much without power as well. Oh, we had an old car alternator mounted on the stern rail, and it was attached by a long piece of rope to an old outboard propeller. If we sailed at eight knots, we might be able to get a few amps out of it, which was just about enough to keep the car battery below decks charged with enough power to run the small VHF radio. We used kerosene lamps for light, and even kerosene running lamps.

The wind had finally started blowing about 11:00 a.m. of the third day. Catalina was still in sight off our stern. As Catalina is just 24 miles from my homeport, that meant we hadn't gone all that far.

But that morning was the day that decided the course for the rest of my life.

The first day out of Redondo, sitting becalmed off the Palos Verdes Peninsula, I started to blow chunks as if I were Mount Vesuvius. By dawn the next morning, my stomach thought my throat was a one-way street going the wrong way! I had nothing left to throw up but my toes.

Yeah, you get the picture. I was seasick as a dog. This was back in about 1978, and it was my first experience with an overnight sail. The first two days were spent trying to decide if I was more afraid I was going to die, or that I wouldn't!

By midday, day two, I had pretty well come to grips with my seasickness. When I was supposed to go on watch, I'd walk up on deck, stick my finger down my throat and perform Olympian feats of projectile spewing. After that, I'd feel pretty good and could actually sit and take my watch for the next couple hours. I might have had to practice a few more times, but all in all, I became accustomed to it.

And then, day three! I had fallen asleep in my bunk after the 2:00 a.m. watch with the porthole open and my face stuck in it to get air. The sun hit me at about 8:00 a.m. and I remembered waking up long enough to roll over and pull the pillow over my face, but I also remembered feeling as if I'd forgotten something. I had. I'd forgotten to get up and try once again to bring my toenails up through the inner route.

When I stumbled out of bed at about 9:30, the boat had stopped the rail-to-rail rocking we'd experienced for the first two days, and it was fairly steady. I walked out onto the deck and Captain Olsen was at the tiller. He smiled and asked how I was. My answer just kind of rolled out. I was fine.

I was! I wasn't feeling sick anymore!

I can't tell you how exciting that was. I walked forward and stood there looking south, south to where God only knows what was to happen. But I felt good.

No, I don't mean I didn't feel sick. I mean I felt good! All of a sudden I realized that I was on the adventure of a lifetime. A day earlier I was thinking with dread that it might be a whole week before I could get off the cursed boat and return to a normal life aground. Now I felt filled with a sense of adventure. I wanted the moment to go on forever; the sound of the sea rushing under the boat; the feel of the wind on my back and the spray of the water all around.

There were no dolphins to welcome me to my new life. They would come later. The skies didn't open up, and a ray of light didn't hit me, but nonetheless, in that instant, standing on the foredeck of an old square-rigged schooner, my life changed forever.

PART 2

Cruising

What is a cruiser?

A friend of mine flew in to say hi after cruising Mexico for the past six months. He's been considered a cruiser around here for as long as I can remember, but this is really the first time he's gotten out there to really cruise long distance.

We have often touched on just what a cruiser really is in the pages of *Latitudes & Attitudes*, and I have to admit, for a lifestyle that I have pretty much devoted the past 30 years to, I can't explain just what a cruiser really is.

So anyway, Jim and I were sitting in my office the day he got back, talking. This, as you well know, is what cruisers do. They talk.

They talk about their cruises, about cruises they are on, about cruises that haven't happened yet, and about cruises that haven't even been planned yet.

The conversation got around to people he'd met while cruising. As he told me of various folks he'd met along the way, I kept thinking back to when I was out there with Jody.

People are what cruising is all about. The various types and characters make up just how much a particular place is either enjoyed, or not enjoyed. As an example, Jim is not a drinker. Not a religious thing, he just doesn't care for what it does to a lot of folks. You know, like the old saying on the T-shirt, "Instant Butthead, just add alcohol."

He was telling me about one boat he met, where the whole voyage was about where the cheapest beer was.

Now I gotta admit, there were many times when we were cruising that we would make a judgment call as to which harbor to pull into based on what we'd heard about the price of a cold one.

But then I thought back to a boat I once moored next to for a few weeks when I was down in Nuevo Vallarta about 16 years ago.

The boat was named MARIPOSA; a beautiful name which means butterfly in Spanish, for what was once probably a beautiful boat. It was a Formosa 41—a Bill Garden design that at one time was my dream boat.

Anyway, we were in a slip next to this guy. Every morning at about 6:00 a.m. we'd hear him slamming his hatch and heading out to the local bar. Late at night, or more realistically in the wee hours of the morning, he'd be slamming the door again, as he came home from the bar. This was his ritual every day.

I don't know what he lived on, and don't really care. What I do know is, about three years later I saw his boat seized in the navy area of the harbor entrance in Puerto Vallarta. When I asked about it I was told the man had died, and the boat was finally hauled off because no one came to claim it or to pay the slip fees.

Now I had talked with this guy, or tried to one day, and he informed me he'd been "cruising" for almost five years. I asked him where he'd been, and he gave me an answer I will never forget.

"Why, I've been here! I found a place I liked and these are my cruising grounds!"

The man did consider himself a cruiser because he lived on a boat, and it wasn't in a slip in his home marina.

I told Jim this, and we sat there trying to define just what it is that makes a cruiser. After a while we concluded that cruising is a state of mind.

It is the adventure of finding a new way of life, the thrill you feel when you are about to depart on a new cruise, whether it is around the world or across the river.

Some people who are "out there" are just boat people. They don't cruise for the fun of cruising, they live on a boat in an inexpensive place because it's cheap.

Jim's boat is on the hard in Mexico as he works here, trying to get enough money to get back out there, where he belongs.

Why? Because he's a cruiser, and that's what cruisers do. It's not where the boat sits that makes a person a cruiser, it's where that person is trying to go.

Cruisers are an odd lot. They travel for the sake of travel itself. They wander the face of the earth in a search, not for a better place, but for a new adventure, a new look at something they have never seen before.

We wander from the heat of the tropics to the freezing cold of the arctic. It's what we do.

All who wander are not lost!

Charts

The changes in sailing and navigation are pretty hard to keep up with. I know that I get pretty confused, and I go to all the boat shows, so I must be more up on this stuff than most of you. Right?

So if I'm as confused about this stuff as I am, you guys got to be climbing the walls. I mean, what is the best form of navigational device?

Is it the new Whazzoo 48-mile color radar with built-in chart plotter and overlay?

Or perhaps it's the new digitized plotters that show not only what a chart represents, but split the screen so you can see the bottom contour and sea-state all at one time?

I was sitting on the LOST SOUL the other day, contemplating my navel or whatever it is we do when we are not trying to fix whatever has broken most recently. I was almost on the edge of boredom as I looked around the main saloon.

I walked over to the saloon table and lifted the lid of the box I'd built to hold charts. I remembered when I'd built it. We had just sailed back from Tonga, and were getting ready to leave for Greece. I had all my chart tubes full of charts for the Pacific, and had no place to put my Atlantic, Caribbean and Mediterranean charts. Then I got this hairbrained idea to build a chart box under the table.

It actually turned out pretty well. Better than I expected. I mounted one of those kewl gas-operated goodies to lift the tabletop, and even put a little light under it, so when you open the table you have light to see what's there, just like in a refrigerator.

I sat down in front of the table and popped it open. All of a sudden, I was no longer bored. There, in front of me, were all the charts and guides that I'd used on my last major voyage. Right there on top was my favorite—the overall chart of the Eastern Pacific.

I used this chart in 1991 when I sailed down to Puerto Vallarta on my initial shakedown cruise. Then again, in 1992, when Jody and I sailed south to Cabo San Lucas, and on to the Marquesas, the Tuamotus and Tahiti.

I followed the little Xs, each one marked with a date, and remembered why we had kinda zigged as we crossed the equator. That day was a short day, and the Xs were very close. That's because we had stopped, right there in the middle of the ocean, for a Shellback Ceremony. All of a sudden I had this big grin on my face, remembering the day.

There were also a series of Xs going from Pago Pago in American Samoa to Christmas Island. The Xs were fairly uniform in distance, because the whole 990-mile voyage was against a 25-30 knot wind, and where it zigged a little was where the equatorial current and the countercurrent were pretty close together.

Sitting there, I remembered the feeling we had inside when we finally spotted the island after almost eight days of being beaten up by the winds and seas.

There were no Xs from the Tuamotus to Tahiti, or Tahiti to Suverov, or to Tonga and Samoa. We'd used smaller charts for that. This chart was just for the crossings.

There were three sets of Xs between Hawaii and California. That was from 1993, when we'd sailed home after Christmas, and our crossing to Hawaii in 2002. Then the other was our last crossing, just 8-10 months ago, when we sailed back here. It was fun checking how close we came to crossing the same point in the ocean, but never quite actually crossing our own path.

And then it hit me. With all the fancy electronic garbage being thrust upon us, how am I going to get this feeling in the future? Looking at an electronic screen?

I think not.

No, the ring from the coffee cup on that paper chart is worth more to me than all the simplifications that the electronic stuff gives me. I remember when it happened. We were four days out of Clarion Island, on our way to the Marquesas. We got side-slapped by a wave and it jarred my cup as I stood there checking our position early one morning.

And the faded spot on the edge of the chart, where a wave dropped through the open hatch soaking part of it, as we were about halfway from Hawaii to Redondo? I didn't find it until I came down to wake Jody for her watch. I remembered thinking we'd better get a new chart when we got home.

But we didn't.

And we won't. Not as long as there is enough to still navigate by. And when we can't use it anymore, I think I'll frame the darn thing.

Try that with a chip!

Mysterious sailor

When I was but a mere youth (pronounced yoo-t), I was always walking because I couldn't drive yet.

When I reached the point in life where I knew more than anyone else (that'd be between 16 and 30), I was always busy playing volleyball on the beach, or working out at the gym, or swimming.

Then came the time in life when I would be traveling, doing a lot of diving and working fairly hard.

Now that I am approaching middle age (middle age is always 15 years older than you are at the time), I find I have to force myself to do stuff so my ticker doesn't quit on me. You know, stuff like walking when it's easier to drive. Like taking the stairs when there's a perfectly good elevator nearby, or swimming to shore when the dinghy works just fine.

What has all this got to do with sailing you might well ask yourself, wondering if at last I have dropped the few screws that were still in my melon?

Well, every morning I am forced by conscience, or by my wife, Jody, to get out of a perfectly warm bed and go out into the cold and walk in ever larger circles.

Over the past few months the circle has ranged a couple of miles, and each morning I dutifully leave LOST SOUL, head up the dock and over the parking lot, along the pathway that follows the channel from our marina.

Each morning I have been noticing this same sailboat, a rather old Catalina 27, sailing out of the harbor.

Now what first caught my attention was that it didn't matter if there was any wind or not. The boat was always drifting under main and headsail. Most days, at that time in the morning there is no wind. Yet here would be the lone sailboat, drifting at half a knot.

One morning my journey from nowhere to nowhere else took me along the seawall about 50 feet from this boat, as it drifted a tad slower than I was walking. I noticed an elderly (that means older than me!) gentleman sitting back, tiller in hand, and I could hear Glenn Miller's Moonlight Serenade wafting across the water to me.

I stopped and stood watching. How kewl was this? How could you get any more enjoyment out of a vessel than this man was getting, sitting back, drifting on his boat, listening to great tunes and watching the world drift by?

I don't know the gentleman who is sailing the boat, though it would be very easy to just follow him to his slip and say "Hi." Actually, I'd rather see him as I picture him in my mind's eye. He could be an old bomber pilot reliving the days of the Big War, or he could be a retired sailor looking back into a life of sailing.

Or he could be an ex-con who just got outta the joint. I don't really want to know. I don't want to ruin the scene I have created in my imagination. To know too much would take away from the stories that I build.

They say reality can never match your imagination, and my imagination has no bounds.

I remember when I was planning my world cruise, walking those same walkways and looking out across the ocean, dreaming the adventures that I would soon be living. And I lived them, and they were good.

So now I enjoy every morning as I walk the torturous steps on the Esplanade, and up the steep ramps that I have set as a goal. And as I walk to stay alive, I look over at my anonymous friend and think through the story of the day.

Was he an itinerant dockworker, working his way from Bombay to Rangoon? Was he once the lead singer for a long forgotten mop-headed group who made it in the 60s? Or perhaps just a retired engineer from TRW. Maybe a retired magazine guy?

It doesn't matter, because in my mind he is what I someday want to be—happiest with just a simple boat and a little breeze!

Fade to black . . .

An hellacious blast of wind gripped the sails and the boat heeled over until I thought we'd be thrown out. I found myself dangling precariously from a chrome goody that spun around, which I later learned was a winch. I looked down into the icy-green water, wishing I had never left terra firma.

"Hey, would you mind easin' the mainsheet a little?" I heard the captain ask, in a very calm voice. I just couldn't imagine how anyone could be calm in a situation where we were obviously about to die. Besides that, what in God's name was a mainsheet?

Fade to grey . . .

I had just finished laying on a coat of high-gloss varnish on the cabin soles of the LOST SOUL. We were tied to a mooring just behind the marina's breakwater, and the sun was painting the sky a myriad of gold and orange that seems to only exist when viewed from the deck of a sailing vessel.

I walked forward and settled into a beanbag I kept on deck for the comfort of any long-legged California deck potato that might happen by. As I really started to enjoy the sunset I heard the soft and mournful wail of a tenor sax wafting across the water. Gary Delugg, who lived on his gaff-rigged double-ender a couple moorings over, was also celebrating the end of the day.

The sun slowly lowered behind the horizon in brilliant bursts of red and orange, just as the last notes of the sax drifted across the still harbor.

A scattering of applause could be heard from the landslugs who had come to watch the sunset, and from the scattering of other people who were on their boats on the moorings.

Fade to grey . . .

I heard a loud crack, and ducked as an 18-foot piece of my toerail broke loose from the boat. The sail-track was through bolted but the rail couldn't stand the stress of a full gale, even with just a storms'l. The wind whipped it around as if it were just a twig.

We were only 180 miles out of Hawaii on the end of a three-week crossing from Mexico, when all of a sudden the winds reversed and we found ourselves going bow-first into a pure hell of white foam horses. We were being blown across a wind-whipped sea of dark, almost black water. Before it ended and the trades returned we would be blown almost 100 miles off course.

Four days later I started to get worried. According to my last noon sight, we should have seen 12,000-foot Mauna Kea.

I anxiously walked the deck, not wanting to worry the rest of the crew, but knowing we should have seen land hours ago.

"Land Ho!"

It was Bruce. He was standing on the bow pulpit, pointing ahead. Unbelievably, we were almost on the island. We could actually see the surf breaking just a few hundred feet in front of us, but no island!

It seemed a volcano had erupted on the other side of

the island that day. We hadn't heard about it, but there was an atmospheric disturbance that allowed less than one-mile visibility on a perfectly clear day.

Fade to grey . . .

The worst thing about firsts is, they can only happen once. One of the beauties of cruising is, there are so many firsts that we still get to experience, in an age when firsts can be appreciated. Your first sail may be behind you, but you can always relive it in your mind, because it will always be a first. The first time you go sailing (scene one), the first day you live aboard (scene two), or the first ocean crossing (scene three) are just a few of these.

How about your first gale? Your first crossing of the equator? The first time you throw a wrench across a room in rage at an inanimate object screaming "I hate boats!" All these things you have to look forward to.

Planning your first cruise. Sitting down with all the charts and guides and info you can find, and living the cruise long before it even starts.

The first time you enter a new harbor will happen literally hundreds of times, and the beauty of this lifestyle is, you can re-live each of these, because each is as vivid in memory as your first true love.

After 30 or 40 years, you will still have firsts to look forward to, because it is impossible to run out of new harbors and new adventures when you cruise. While your friends will be living vicariously through your letters, you will be living each day, each adventure.

*   *   *

The sun broke out from behind the black clouds, and all of a sudden the rain and squall of the darkest storm of the cruise melted into a warm and beautiful day. Just then we spotted Nuku Hiva, our first tropical island.

Fade to black . . .

Blush on the rose refit

I finally made one of the toughest decisions I have
had to make regarding my boat, and it took me over
a year to make it.

Every boater goes through the same process. You got a
boat that you've had for a while, and you know every little
defect in the darn thing.

On the LOST SOUL, after 14 years and over 75,000 miles,
there was no spot on the boat where I could stand and not
see something that I wanted to fix or change.

What was odd was that other people would come
aboard and ooh and aah all over her, but all I could see was
what needed to be fixed or changed.

And so it was that, a little over a year ago, I talked Jody
into putting her on the market and starting to look for another home.

Since I have lived aboard for almost 30 years, I am
pretty particular about what I want in a boat. I know all the
little things that make a boat a home.

So we put her on the market and started looking. It
didn't take long until we found there were no boats like the
LOST SOUL being built any more. Well, there could be, but
the cost was way prohibitive. It would have to be custom
built, and after talking with my friend Bob Perry, I realized
I couldn't afford it.

So we looked at what was available in something we could

afford. At every boat show we would walk the docks, and I have to admit I did find a few that we could have lived on. The Hylas 54 and the Moody were candidates, as well as the new Gozzard. They were all the type of boat we were looking for; large enough to live on, easy to handle, and strong enough for a world cruise.

And each time, after we'd sit on these great new boats, we would think, "Yeah, we could do this."

Sitting on a new, well-laid-out boat takes your worries and throws them into a bait bucket. You don't have to worry that your tanks might start leaking. The LOST SOUL is 23 years old and has black iron tanks. We already had to fix two of the four tanks!

And the wiring! Beautiful color-coded wiring, with every wire in its right loom, and each one labeled and tagged, with beautiful new 12-volt and 110 panels, with cute little lights that glow when the switch is activated. Compare this to our mishmash of wiring that has been done and re-done 20 times, sometimes at sea, and always in a hurry. Every wire is red, because we got a special on 100 pounds of red wire back when we were first refitting the boat. Lots of dead wire, and wires leading nowhere.

And then walk the new teak decks. They feel so firm under foot. The caulking is perfect, and they use the new pressure applied system with no screws to work loose and create leaks. Not like our decks that are a tad on the spongy side, and caulking that has been re-done more often than Tammy Fay's makeup and looks just as bad.

And then there is the fact that they are dry! The LOST SOUL has only a couple of leaks, but I gotta tell ya, I have traced them for almost 15 years and been unsuccessful in locating the source of these mystery leaks.

And then the show is over and we head home. We board our baby and it is like walking into a womb. She surrounds us with warmth, and she feels solid, and every little nook and cranny has a memory and a story to tell. It is our home. The others are more like hotels to us.

And so we sat and we thought. Just what are the problems that we want to get rid of in order to be happy? A list was started. As we added to that list, we started to feel relieved. All of a sudden it was like we'd made the decision. Everything we liked about the other boats was listed first, and what it would take to make our baby have the same good things. We listed everything that was wrong, no matter how slight, and then we tried to figure what it would cost to make our true love into as good a condition as a new boat.

And so it was, we started on the list. The major things that actually put fear into our hearts weren't all that bad (in theory!). We wanted easier sail handling, so we ordered Leisurfurl In-Boom Furling. The leaks that bugged us were in the pilot house, so we started a complete re-build of that structure. Teak decks a little soft? We will rip them off and re-glass, and then re-teak the decks.

The wiring? That threw us, but then I bit the bullet and we started to tear out all the wiring on the boat, and will be re-wiring like a new boat. Stem to stern.

At this point (the start) we are both very optimistic. As the project develops, we'll see. But for now we are very excited.

We'll see just how long the blush stays on that rose!

The perfect cruising boat

What is the perfect cruising boat? I don't know how many times I've been asked that question. The answer is, there's no such animal. Unequivocally, period.

Now there are people out there who really like what they have, but, if you'll notice, they are always in a state of flux.

Did you ever meet a boater who wasn't working on something to make his boat better? Of course not. It's a way of life.

I remember about 15 years ago, when I had a boat I was pretty much happy with. I didn't have any projects going. No improvements in mind. I was just sailing it and enjoying it. Her name was PREDATOR, and she was a Formosa 51.

Right about now performance cruisers are champing at the bit. "A Formosa 51! It won't get out of its own way!" they shout. "It won't sail tighter than 50° on the weather!" they scream.

Yeah. So, what's your point? Maybe I didn't want to go fast. Back in those days I had plenty of time to get there, so I was happy.

But one afternoon I was sailing into port, feeling pretty spiffy, as we turned on the wind and dropped the sails smartly. Billy Jack dropped the headsail, Gina dropped the mizzen and I dropped the main, like clockwork. We were looking goood! We had spent the previous week laying on some varnish, and the stainless gleamed.

As it turned out, we were looking a little too good. Unbeknownst to us, there was a gentleman having a late lunch at the Lighthouse restaurant, with his broker. He'd flown in from Alaska looking for a boat, and hadn't found one. Until he saw PREDATOR.

The broker met us on the dock.

"Hey, do you want to sell that boat?" he asked.

Well, you know how it is, you never say no to a question like that. If you're happy with your boat at the time, you just jack the price up. Everything's got a price, right?

"Yeah, sure." I said, and I named an exorbitant price. Twice what I'd paid for the boat just a year earlier.

"Mind if I show my client?" he asked.

A half hour later I was standing scratching my head, wondering what had taken place. I had sold my boat. It was Sunday, and we would haul for survey on Monday. If all went well, I would have a week to vacate.

I was happy. Two weeks later I was moving onto a brand new 42-foot performance cruiser. It had less than an hour's worth of teak, could be singlehanded by any dolt, even me! Below decks it was pristine and simple. Kewl! I named her ASSAILANT, and took off on our maiden voyage.

Three months later I was shopping for another Taiwan Turkey. Sure ASSAILANT was fast. Yeah, she was easy to handle. There was almost no maintenance, and she almost maintained herself. The perfect boat, right?

No way, dude! She had about as much personality and character as a tupperware container. It wasn't until late one night, I was in my dinghy after an evening doing 12-ounce curls at the Harbor Lounge. I was looking for my boat and I realized, I didn't recognize it. My boat looked just like everyone else's! Ah!

As most folks know, I did find a project. The LOST SOUL. My friends thought I'd slipped a gear or two. To sell a new, perfect boat, and buy one that is closer to sinking than not. It was just crazy. But the first moment I walked onto her teak decks, complete with missing caulking and bent stanchions, I was home.

And then I realized the truth of the situation. There is no perfect boat. There is just the boat that's right for you. How do you know it? What do you look for? Well, as soon as you step aboard it feels like home. Logic doesn't enter into it, though logical we all strive to be when looking.

Part of the joy I get from cruising includes those days when I stand screaming "I hate boats!"

So the next time you see a neighbor, shirt all greasy, blood dripping from a wounded paw that got hooked on an old cotter key (yeah, it happens to us all), pity him not. Know that, in reality, this is the fun part.

Remember this. The harder the battle, the more heartfelt the victory.

I'll see ya. I'm gonna go work on my boat!

Depth of feelings

▶◀

You've just pulled out of Gibraltar and headed around the southern tip, on your way to Ibiza, Spain. Your significant other is down below, and you're on watch. You stand holding the wheel watching the ships that squeeze through the bottleneck at the Strait of Gibraltar, and wonder, "How many centuries have men felt this wonder?" In front of you is all the history you have read about, and you are about to discover it for yourself, at your own pace. An unsurpassed feeling of anticipation fills you.

The boat is going to right itself. The fifty-foot wave that just broke over you slammed you down a bit, but the boat took it, and is popping back up just like it's supposed to. You tighten the main sheet to where it should be, and check the reef lines. Everything is okay. You holler down to the crew below that it's over, and then it hits you.

What if the wave had been bigger? What if the stays'l hadn't held? The mast could have broken! Or the keel bolts broken off! What then? The boat would have capsized. And what if the safety harness hadn't kept you in place when the wave hit, or, God forbid, what if you hadn't put it on? Look behind you. There is nothing back there, and you wouldn't have been missed for an hour or so. At least until the next person was going to come on watch. Can you imagine what that would be like? Treading water and watching the boat sail off without you?

It always seems to come after the worst is over. During the storms, the ordeals, or the tight reef entrances. But when it's over, that's when it hits you. Fear! Gut-wrenching fear!

You were supposed to arrive in the Marquesas after 22 days, and here you are, pulling in after just 18 days. The storms that pushed you were hell. The rain seemed to find every place that leaked on the boat, and you were really getting pretty tired of trying to find a dry spot in the bunk.

Beans and cold stew had been your meal more nights than you might have wanted, and the autopilot going out at the halfway point didn't help much either.

But there, in front of you. Nuku Hiva! Look at the spires. The harbor looks like heaven. More colors of blue in the water and more colors of green on the hills than you even imagined, and you are here on your own boat.

You've done it! As you look at the small tear in the mainsail, a feeling sweeps over you. You prepared your boat to the best of your ability. You planned for the storms, and the fuses that went out, and the wet weather.

And now you are pulling into your first South Pacific paradise under your own power. The storms, the seas, the 2,800 miles behind you seem like nothing. You can't help but smile, as you wave to a passing cruiser who is heading out of the channel.

"Yeah!" You say to yourself, almost aloud. "Yeah, I made it. The boat made it. The crew made it. And only a handful of people on earth can ever say they have accomplished such a feat."

The feeling is so strong you almost feel a chill.

Pride. The pride of conquering unknown dangers to accomplish a goal.

The squall hit late at night. Your wife was on watch, and she hesitated to wake you, but the sails had to be reefed, and it takes two.

Since she's on watch she feels it's her place to go out and handle the reef lines, so you turn the boat into the wind to let the sail luff, and watch as she ties each line. All the miles behind you, and she still has the same feeling for the boat. And for the lifestyle.

She finishes tying the lines and gives the high sign. Everything is okay. You turn downwind to fill the sails, and adjust the sheet line. The rain is coming down hard now, and as you look up you see her walking between the house and the lifelines.

It had been warm on her watch, so she was wearing a bathing suit. Then the rain hit so she has a poncho on. You look up from the winch and she's standing there, rain running down her face, with the biggest grin you've ever seen. Your heart melts.

Love. Pure and simple.

There is no other lifestyle on this water-planet that can evoke such feelings, such depth of emotion, as cruising. The challenges that meet you only make them stronger. Being in charge of your own destiny becomes a way of life, and most cruisers find, if they ever stop cruising, that they can't return to their old lifestyle. But then again, who the hell would want too?

And there you are

━━━━▶◀━━━━

*L*and was only four or five miles in front of me. It had to be. That I couldn't see anything out there didn't alter that fact. It had to be there.

Of course I couldn't tell the other four people on board I didn't know where we were. They were counting on me. I was the captain, and if I let them know I wasn't sure, they would probably get nervous. Like I was.

We'd left Cabo San Lucas, Mexico, 18 days earlier. The crossing had been great. Everything I had ever hoped for. The farther we got away from land, the better the winds, the warmer the weather and the more I liked it.

My crew consisted of my 18-year-old girlfriend (hey, I was single back then, so it's okay!) and her girlfriend from Minnesota, my friend Bruce, a bodybuilder who worked at a gym I owned, and a young man who'd just graduated from the Law School at the University of Colorado.

We were using a sextant to find our way, shooting noon sights daily. About halfway across we spotted a super-tanker named Bass Pike, and they were kind enough to inform me that I was about 800 miles from where I thought we were.

Oops!

After an hour of checking I found my mistake. I had been adding the declination instead of subtracting. Each day my error compounded on itself. This was before GPS and I couldn't afford a Sat/Nav back then, as they cost about $2,000.

Once I corrected my mistake and we knew our new position, I was sure we were fine. After all, the sailing directions to get to Hawaii were simple. Sail south until the butter melts, then go west until you hear the ukuleles.

About 150 miles out of Hawaii we were hit on the nose with a Kona storm, 45-55 knots of wind out of the southwest. We were blown 100 miles back in two days and blew out our toerail. What fun.

Anyway, after the storm was over we made good time and sailed toward the big island.

So here we were. As I figured it, about three-four miles from the Big Island. Mauna Kea and Mauna Loa raise over 12,000 feet from the ocean. They'd be as easy to see as Liz Taylor's butt in bright red Spandex.

To this point I had been trying to sail the old fashioned way. I had a radio direction finder (RDF) on board, but didn't want to use it. I wanted to get there like my ancestors had. Just with the stars and the sun to guide me.

After looking at the chart and seeing how big the ocean is, and how small the islands, I decided discretion was the better part of valor and broke out the RDF.

I found a station in Waikiki on Oahu, and then I found one in Hilo, on the Big Island of Hawaii. I put an "X" where the position indicated. It coincided with where I had figured I was.

So where was the 12,000-foot peak?

With much trepidation, I decided I should let my crew in on the fact that I was a dunderhead and had gotten us about as lost as I could. The aptness of my vessel's name was all too apparent at the time. LOST SOUL, yup, that'd be us!

I walked up on deck feeling about as low as a snake's ass in a wagon track.

I called the crew together on the aft deck. They all looked at me as trusting as puppies looking at their mother. As I was figuring out how I would tell them the news that I had really let them down, I heard a motor in the distance.

I looked up and saw a most incongruous sight for a boat lost at sea. It was an old Chris-Craft speedboat pulling a most attractive lady on water skis behind.

I waved them over, and they made a pass by the boat.

"Hey, where's Hilo?" I screamed.

They made a long and slow turn, and made another pass. As they did, the skipper of the boat pointed right in front of us.

"'Bout two miles that way, Brah!" I heard him holler.

The crew started to cheer. I just stood there, stunned. Two miles? How could that be? It was a clear day and we couldn't see any land or anything.

I sent the girls up to the bow and had Bruce climb up to the first spreaders. As he was turning to look, we all saw it at once. Breakers on a white sand beach. We were less than a mile offshore.

Then it all started to come together. The depth sounder showed 500 feet. We could hear the surf and we had completed our first ever ocean crossing.

After we landed we found out that the Kilauea volcano had erupted (that was 1983) and caused a weird atmospheric condition. Visibility was down to less than half a mile on a clear day.

This goes to prove a very valuable lesson. As my old friend Glenn Stewart used to say, "No matter where you go, there you are."

Peter Island boat

➤◄

We were anchored in Little Harbor, on Peter Island in the British Virgin Islands. After a cruise through the USVI, we'd just spent a quick five days visiting old friends on various boats and islands in this area, and for our last night we decided to just tuck in to a nice natural anchorage and enjoy the cruising.

Anchored here in the bay were about a dozen boats. No stores here, no bars to get crazy at. Just a beautiful blue bay with a couple of white sand beaches and some good snorkeling. Pretty much perfection for a cruiser.

We dove in for a quick swim to cool off after anchoring. Shortly after we got out of the water I noticed a very small boat that had been anchored up against the shore. It looked to be about 26 to 30 feet, had a black hull, and was a gaff-rigged sloop; the kind of boat that will bring a lump into the throat of any long-time sailor.

As I watched I noticed the man on board climb into a small rowing dinghy and row to the shore, untying the line he'd run there to keep him stern to the beach. What kept my attention was how slow and deliberate every move he made was. As if he'd pre-thought every step, and it was like second nature to him.

Jody walked up on deck and sat down, and we continued to watch the poetry of motion on this small, beautiful vessel.

He tied the dinghy off on his stern and walked to the mast. There he took the gaskets off and hoisted the gaff-rigged, tan bark main. He was close in to a lee shore, and the wind was pretty much non-existent, but that didn't seem to bother him.

Every move he made was slow and deliberate. He walked to the bow and started to pull in his anchor chain, hand over hand. As he did he flaked it onto the deck in neat rows. When the hook came out of the water he looked around to be sure he was not drifting into shore, or to another boat, and then he tied down the anchor and stowed his chain. Slowly. Thoughtfully. Perfectly.

He walked to his port rail and pulled out what looked like a long pole. We were a little ways out, but I soon recognized it as a very long oar. It looked to be about 15 feet long. He walked back to the stern with it, and stuck it into a slot that was made for it. Then he started to slowly scull his boat away from shore with the oar.

After a few deft strokes the vessel started a forward motion. We sat spellbound by the perfection of every move. He left the oar in the oarlock and walked forward to the headsail, deftly pulling his headsail up. He stopped and watched to see how it was filling. He then walked back to the main boom and pushed it out by hand, holding it to catch the wind. The headsail started to billow with a little breeze.

As the beautiful little sloop started moving out I felt a kinship with this man I was watching—this man I'd never met and might never know—a respect, and maybe even a little envy. It was obvious that this man had a relationship with his vessel that men have had for generations, the feelings evoked by reading Irving Johnson, Sterling Hayden and Tristan Jones.

Oh, there were plenty of fancy new fiberglass boats stern tied around the harbor, and a lot of us knew how to back in with our engines and do everything that has to be done to attain a safe mooring, but none of us seemed to have the same relationship with our home and our environment as this sailor did.

As the wind filled the sails I saw him stow his sculling oar, walk to the stern and take his tiller in hand. I could almost feel the exhilaration he had to feel as I watched his vessel pull out of the lee. I "felt" his sails fill, and I could feel the boat start to pull into the trades.

I took a photo as this gallant little gaff-rigged sloop sailed out of the harbor. I used it on the cover of an issue of *Latitudes & Attitudes.* Every once in a while something affects you, in a moment, in a split second, that can and will change your life. For me it happened almost 30 years ago when I first set eyes on the square-rigged topsail schooner, STONEWITCH, on board which I had the honor of sailing.

Hopefully, the photo on the cover of the magazine will affect some young sailor just starting to enter into this lifestyle, and 35-40 years from now, he will capture a similar moment which he will pass on.

Five hundred years ago a young Chris Columbus was so inspired. Three hundred years ago it was a lad named Nelson.

Perhaps a couple of hundred years from now, someone who sees this photo, being so inspired, will become a sailing legend as well!

Joys of varnishing

———————►◄———————

Varnishing. Yuck! It's got to be one of the toughest jobs on a boat like LOST SOUL. As you apply the expensive slime, it must go through your alleged mind that you will be doing the same thing in just a few months or it will all be for naught.

Then why is it that I like or maybe even love varnishing? I miss it when I get too busy and have to hire someone to put a coat on, and actually feel a little jealous that they get to be standing out there, sweating in the sun, varnishing.

For me the application of varnish is more like therapy than work. I well remember days when we were cruising, anchored off a sand beach, lovingly caressing the teak rail of my boat with a ham-sized paw cupping some 220-grit paper, smoothing the surface for a coat of the golden elixir that turns a man's boat into his own piece of living art.

I love the way the surface turns from a milky white to a brilliant shine when I rub it down with fresh water to check for places I might have missed. I actually got to a point where we would break the varnishing down into manageable areas that we'd do on a weekly basis, rather than doing it all at once about every three months. My crew thought it was because I was trying to keep up with the job. I don't think they ever really knew that it was because I actually enjoyed the job of varnishing. They'd have thought I was nuts, which has a high probability of truth in it.

What it is for me is one of the few ways a person can get almost instant gratification every time you do it.

You wake up in the morning anchored in Moorea after a three-month crossing from Mexico to the Marquesas, and then through the Tuamotus and on to Tahiti. In Papeete you spend all your time running around in circles doing the clearance dance, and then you shop till you drop, or your Visa card maxes out. It's almost (not quite!) like work.

And then you look at your port rail. It's crusted with salt, and you can barely recognize the beautiful shining teak rail that it was the day you last varnished.

And so, you get comfortable standing in the dink and wipe it down with fresh water. It starts to look a little better.

For the next couple of hours you caress the surface with some 220-grit paper working your way from one end to the other. On occasion you hit a bad spot and whip out a little 100 grit, smoothing that spot where the anchor chain dropped a little too hard, or where you bumped into the fuel dock in Cabo.

After you wipe it down with fresh water you go over it with a tack rag to pull all the last vestiges of dust off. Then you are ready.

Laying the varnish on is the epitome of the gratification process; watching the somewhat dull surface all of a sudden come alive with a brilliance and color that only the teak rail of a sailing vessel can achieve.

Laying it on and keeping a wet edge is an art that can only be achieved with time and infinite patience. Watching as the bristles of the badger brush lay down a smooth, yet slightly wavy texture, and then the gravity and warmth of the sun smooth that texture into a glassy brilliance, it's almost mesmerizing.

And all too soon you have reached the other end of the rail. It's finished.

You make your way around to the opposite side of the boat to board and go below. It's almost a religious thing for me. Don't look at the finished project for at least 30 minutes, until the surface has started to harden. Then, and only then, is when the true instant gratification sets in as you look at what was once a salt-covered and dull ship's rail. It has been transformed by your will and the sweat of your brow into something that you can take pride in.

For years I had read of how people have painted all the surfaces of their boats so they didn't have to perform maintenance like varnishing and cleaning. I have never understood that and still don't.

I think a big part of what I enjoy about the cruising lifestyle is the way I feel about my boat as I enter a harbor. No matter how hard fought the battle to make it to a port, on arrival the sails are stowed, the decks are clear, and we always try to make it look as if we are just coming in from a daysail.

One of the biggest joys of having a boat is having a vessel you are proud of. As I approach my boat in the dinghy I love to look at the varnished rail and the way the sun glints off it. Not because of how it looks to others. That doesn't mean much. It's what I feel inside. It's the way it makes me feel. That's what makes it all the more fulfilling.

It's almost, but not quite, as good as I feel under sail!

Taking responsibility

————————►◄————————

*W*ithin the past few months there have been a bunch of sea-related stories on the news that have made me want to shrivel up and deny I am a sailor. I guess I've just been back in civilization too long.

Why, you ask?

Well, it's simple. So many people are getting into this way of life with absolutely no notion of what it means to take the responsibilities for their own actions. You know . . . like when we were young, the good old scouts motto: be prepared.

I watched one TV story concerning the Coast Guard. Seems someone was suing them for not saving their family when they were involved in a shipwreck during a storm.

Suing them for not saving someone? When you get on a boat and sail off into the sunset you are taking the responsibility to preserve your own life, and those of the people who have trusted their lives to your care. That means you have to be ready for emergencies, not be ready to call for help.

Oh, don't get me wrong. I am not saying you shouldn't call for help. What I am saying is you should be prepared to handle emergencies.

I won't go into particulars about what happened. It was a tragedy, as people died. But to sue the Coast Guard for not rescuing them makes no sense at all.

•••

I have participated in multiple rescues of cruising boats in danger, and seen the Coast Guard go so far beyond their duty as to render them heroes in anyone's book.

I recall in 1994, the yacht CINNAMON rolled and lost its mast halfway from Hawaii to the mainland, 1,000 miles offshore. Yet the Coast Guard, upon hearing of the plight, sent a nearby fuel tanker to give them fuel, monitored them every day, and flew a plane out to drop needed supplies numerous times, escorting them in the last few hundred miles.

In 1995, in a Tehuantepecer storm off Central America, a vessel we were about 300 miles away from called a Mayday. The Coast Guard station in Maine heard the call, passed it to the Naval Air Station in Panama, who sent a plane to help.

In the northwest, three Coasties lost their lives attempting to save the lives of a small crew aboard a sailboat, in seas no one should have been out in. These stories go on and on.

I have never heard of an event at sea where someone has asked for help from the Coast Guard and not received it. I am sure I will now hear from people who have. That's not my point. The point is, because of lawsuits like this, the Coast Guard will now be forced to go more by the book. They will be told to stick to procedure in case someone might want to sue them. As I see it, this will do nothing but worsen the relationship between sailors and Coasties.

I, for one, hate to see that happen.

If you go out on a boat, you are taking your life in your hands. Yeah, it's fun. It's supposed to be, and I would be the last one to tell anyone it isn't. But that doesn't mean you have to be stupid to have fun. Once you are sure you have a good rescue plan for emergencies, and that you have the right equipment on board to be prepared in an emergency, have a ball. But you must be prepared to take the responsibility for your actions.

We have all heard the stories about people taking off without the proper preparation, and if we hear about them and all came through safely, we laugh. I recall one man who was saved with his three children. They had left San Diego to sail to Hawaii. The man thought it was just on the other side of Catalina, some 20-30 miles away, and left with a week's food aboard, for what would actually have been a 2,500-mile, month-long crossing. They were on a 22-foot boat and ended up 500 miles off the coast of Northern California, near death. His comment when rescued? He was planning to go back and get the boat (it was left drifting at sea!) as soon as he was better, and try it again.

Folks, the United States Coast Guard is not there for our use. They are there to guard the coast. We, as sailors, must take it upon ourselves to prepare our vessels so we do not need assistance. That's why it is one of the last vestiges of true freedom. And if we don't start taking care of ourselves, our bungling lawmakers, in their infinite wisdom, will do the task for us.

I, for one, do not want the majority to make a bunch of laws to protect me from my blunders. I feel I am capable of taking care of myself. If you don't feel the same, you shouldn't be sailing in water deeper than you can walk back to shore in.

If I don't return from a voyage, it will either be due to old age or stupidity, but in either case, it will be my own.

Have what you want?

―――――►◄―――――

I woke up to the tinkling of water against the hull of the LOST SOUL, and as I came out of my stupor I remembered where I was. Anchored in Pago Pago, American Samoa. We'd been there about a week, and were planning on leaving in a few days. I pulled on my shorts and walked out of my aft cabin into the galley and threw on a pot of coffee. While I waited for it to brew I went up onto the deck to see what kind of day I could expect. The sun was shining and it was hot, a typical day in the tropics.

As I surveyed my surroundings I saw a new boat had come in during the night. Did I say boat? More like a dream. She sat at anchor a few hundred yards from where I was. A traditional sailing ketch, but larger than any I had ever seen. A hundred and forty feet on deck. A beautiful dark blue hull etched with gold leaf. The brass work was blinding and the varnish was pretty much the same. Wow! What a dream boat. I wanted it. She was on her maiden voyage out of New Zealand.

A few years later I learned that her state-of-the-art carbon fiber masts had broken off shortly after our encounter in Samoa, and she had been laid up in the yard a long time for a refit. This happened while I was on my way to Tonga, on my trusty old boat.

When we were leaving Tonga a few weeks later, we stopped in Niuatoputapu, the northernmost Tongan Islands.

While there we ran into some folks that were trying to raise a schooner that had sunk in the channel a few months earlier. It turns out that the boat they were trying to raise was GOLDEN DAWN, a 103-foot three-masted schooner that I had tried to buy just before I found the LOST SOUL, and wanted so bad I could taste it, but was unable to afford it. Now she lay on the bottom, off a remote island in the South Pacific, while I sailed my trusty old boat away and into the sunset.

Over the ensuing years, as I cruised the world, there were many times when I would see something that I "just had to have." But somehow I didn't get these things. And after a while I learned from these experiences something that has made my life a whole lot easier.

Back in my "buy everything" days, when I had a house and a garage, I just had to have all the stuff. A better car, a bigger TV, a louder stereo, the latest clothes, the fastest motorcycle, and of course, the biggest boat. After moving aboard, over 25 years ago, I realized just what all that crap was worth. Zilch! For over fifteen years I stored it in a garage, while I sailed the world. After returning to that garage a few years ago I had a huge garage sale. I realized none of that stuff had any meaning. Oh, yeah, there were a ton of photos I kept, and the first printings of the books I've written, and copies of the hundreds of magazines I wrote for; but in all, nothing else meant anything anymore.

To put this into a vernacular that all can understand, it's kinda like dating. When you find someone who fits into your lifestyle and becomes a part of your life, you opt for a long-term relationship. Yeah, you'll see a sleek beauty now and then and appreciate her form and beauty, but that doesn't mean you have to own 'em all. You are much happier with your life if you find the right one, and enjoy her to the fullest, while watching the others sail by.

I learned to relate that lesson to boats. Yeah, there are eye-popping models out there, and when I see them I appreciate what I see. Many are sleeker than the LOST SOUL. Most are faster, all have something that I like, because I appreciate boats. But I am attached to my boat. When I approach her from shore I feel a swelling inside when I first spot her. When I am aboard I love the way she feels. I know every flaw, and have learned to not only live with them, but they have become a part of what makes her special.

I have learned a very important lesson from all of this. I am happy with my boat. I appreciate every flaw and nuance, every leak and every imperfect line. Even when I see a newer style sail by, I feel a comfort with what I have.

It is far more important to want the things that you have, than to get the things you want!

When to fly the Jolly Roger

*I*t started on the *Latitudes & Attitudes* Bulletin Board. Someone posted the question, "Are there any issues with flying the Jolly Roger? A scruffy guy in a rowboat told me that the Coast Guard would board my vessel if I fly the ol' skull and crossbones."

This posting was followed by about a dozen posts of boaters discussing what the legalities are surrounding the Jolly Roger.

Okay, come on now. Anyone besides me see the humor in this? Asking permission to fly the Jolly Roger? That would be like a guy asking his mom if it's okay to get a tattoo, or a young woman asking dad if it's okay to bonk her boyfriend.

Flying the Jolly Roger makes me smile when I look up on the mast and see it there. It's a form of rebellion (albeit a very small one) and I do it to feel good. If I had to ask permission, it would be more of an embarrassment.

Any idea where I buy my pirate flags? Would you believe at the "Pirates of the Caribbean" ride at Disney World?

Yup! I stand in line behind a bunch of six-year-olds to buy the best damn pirate flag I can find.

Now tell me, would the man who wouldn't let Annette Funicello bare her bellybutton in the beach movies sell something that was less than all-American?

I think not!

I am writing this the week before the movie *Pirates of the Caribbean* is to be released. By the time you read this it will be history. By the time you read this I have little doubt that it will have set new records for attendance. I am also sure that some enterprising fast food store will be giving out pirate flags as premiums with every burger. It's the way of the world.

Come to think of it, by the time this gets into print, I imagine flying a Jolly Roger will have taken on a whole new meaning. It could even turn into a sign of conformity.

I can see it now . . . cars packed on the freeway, all flying the Jolly Roger from their little plastic window-mounted flag poles. There won't be a boat out there without a pirate flag.

Remember when wearing your hair long was a sign of rebellion? The next time you're at a public function, look around. Only the most conservative now wear long hair. The rebels are shaving their heads. What's up with that? My head's way to ugly to shave. I just wear it bald under my hair.

Sailing is my way of getting into a world where I don't have to be a rebel to do things my way. Out there, not to sound too corny or anything, I am the captain of my own destiny. I know that I have to be responsible for my own actions. Because of that, when I am cruising I feel a freedom that very few of the landbound will ever know. I make decisions based on what I feel is right, and if I have made the wrong decision, I know I have to accept the consequences.

No one tells me when I should or shouldn't have a cold beer when I am cruising. I know when I should, and I know when I shouldn't. It doesn't take a genius to know what's right and wrong.

But what happens is, landbound people are so used to being told what they should or shouldn't do, they actually get to a point where they just can't make the decision for themselves.

That's why we have to get out there in our boats. Being responsible for your own actions means knowing why you don't leave a harbor without a radio. Knowing why you don't drink when you are responsible for other people's lives. We don't have to be told. We just know.

And we just know when to fly the Jolly Roger.

Ha! It's getting too hard to be a rebel anymore!

Life out there is a dream

W e were in the BVIs sailing from Jost Van Dyke to
Virgin Gorda. Just as we were rounding the Dogs,
which is a particularly picturesque small group of rocks
and minuscule islands, I suddenly realized that I didn't
want to get to Virgin Gorda. I didn't want the voyage to end.

So, I turned off the autopilot and swung the rudder until
we were sailing between Cockroach Island and George Dog.
We sailed around for a few more hours, just kind of enjoying the day, and then, just before sunset, we entered Gorda
Sound and headed over to the Bitter End Yacht Club for the
evening.

It was a good day.

We were sailing to Hiva Oa in the Marquesas and had
timed to arrive in a small bay on the north shore, Hana-
menu, just before sunset. We would have made it except we
got a clog in our fuel system and the engine shut down
about five miles out.

But that was okay. We had time, so we started the
bleeding procedures only to find a bad fuel line.

But that was okay, we had a spare fuel line. So, we took
off the old line and replaced it. But in doing so we busted
the nipple.

But that was okay, as we had a spare nipple, so we
replaced it.

But by the time we'd finished, it was almost dark and there was a squall on the horizon.

So, we motored hard and fast, and soon the squall hit us and gave us some wind. So, we motorsailed as fast as we could to make this landfall in a strange harbor before dark.

We didn't make it.

In fact, as we hit the entrance to the bay the squall started to dump biblical amounts of water on our heads. So much so that we couldn't see the bow.

But that was okay, we had radar. Of course it was down below, so we had to steer down in the pilothouse where you couldn't see anything.

It wasn't a very good day.

The LOST SOUL was just finishing a Pacific crossing from Hawaii to California. We had been cruising the previous year in the South Pacific, and we were returning to Redondo Beach to do a little refitting before taking off for the Med, and to piss off our friends by telling them, "No, we're not staying. We just stopped in to say hello!"

As we spotted San Miguel Island, the outermost island in the Channel Islands' chain, Jody and I were sitting on the foredeck as the autopilot, Otto, handled the steering chores. The sun was coming up and for the first time in two years, we were looking at the coastline of California.

"Can't we just keep going?" Jody asked.

I thought for a moment. Was there any way we could? I started searching for some way to justify sailing all this way, and then just saying "the hell with it," and turn south.

I couldn't, we didn't, and we sailed on in.

It was a good day.

*   *   *

It's a five-day sail from Mopelia in the Society Islands to Suverov in the Northern Cooks. The pilot charts said it would be a downwind sail, and we believed them.

Eighty miles out of Mopelia we start getting a head wind (of course!). Soon it builds to 30 knots. Then the clouds come. Pretty soon we look like reruns of the crew of the SS MINNOW as Gilligan took the wheel.

I swear I saw Noah pass us one evening, and for five days we made our four-day crossing against the wind, with every leak in the boat running at full flow. As we entered Suverov there was not a dry towel, blanket or mattress on board.

It was not a good day.

You have all heard the saying that you have to take the bad with the good. I think in cruising we have to take that one step further. As time goes by, you learn to enjoy the bad with the good.

The scenarios I used here are all pretty much etched in my mind. And I look back on all of them and smile. The good, the bad, and the ugly. They stand out in my memory more vividly than all of the days that happened between.

Yeah, the bad days seemed real bad at the time, but now, years later, they are good memories.

And so, now, when the bad days come along, I inwardly grin, knowing that someday in the not too distant future, I will be telling the story of the bad day and enjoying it.

Remember this. When you are in civilization looking at those days out there, you think it was a dream.

When you are out there and think about your life in civilization, it's more like a nightmare.

And there you have it!

Life out there is like a dream, and life when you are back here is more like a nightmare!

PART 3

Attitude

Attitude

———►◄———

*M*any years ago my friend Dr. Larry Hazen told me, "Attitude is the difference between an ordeal and an adventure." In the years since, he has cruised the world and loved every bit of it. Never has a saying held more truth. Put two people on a boat and let them set sail across an ocean. After the storms and high seas and squalls that will inevitably hit are history and the boat arrives at its destination, one of them will say how awful it was because of the bad weather and storms, while the other will be ecstatic after experiencing one of the best adventures of his life. The difference? Attitude. Nothing more.

An acquaintance was a yacht broker in my harbor; she saved for years with her boyfriend to go cruising. They lived aboard their Sea Wolf 41 ketch and put every dollar into outfitting it with the best equipment. One summer they had enough to head out, and they did.

A month later they arrived in Cabo San Lucas, Mexico, some 800 miles south of their departure port. They sold their boat and moved to Colorado. The letter they sent of the trip south sounded like an ordeal from hell: gales off of Cedros Island, untenable anchorages and constant winds over 25 knots. It was awful. It was also typical weather for that area, and everyone heading south experiences the same. I can recall the thrill the first time my old Formosa 51 hit 11 knots in the gale off Cedros. What an adventure!

•••

It's easy to understand their problem. They had done all their sailing around their homeport, where, when the wind would blow over 20 knots, the small craft warnings would go up. They sailed in 10-15 miles per hour of wind and three- to four-foot seas. All of a sudden they were in the Pacific trades. Twenty-five to 30 miles per hour is standard. Seven- to eight-foot seas are the norm. They weren't mentally prepared.

In other words they had left with a wrong attitude!

Before you set sail be sure it's what you want to do. What I recommend is to join friends who are cruising if possible, or to charter a few times to make sure before you sell everything you own and sail off into the sunset, only to come home disillusioned a short time later.

Cruising is a great adventure if you have the right attitude, and an ordeal if you don't.

Sailors have more fun than people

>━━━━━━━►◄━━━━━━━

F or the past few weeks Jody and I have had to move
off the boat, as we are doing some major projects
that pretty much make it impossible to live aboard. This is
the first time in over 13 years for Jody, and almost 30 years
for me.

It has been an eye-opener. Since we started *Latitudes &
Attitudes* we have been doing a little cartoon on the first
page of the Scuttlebutt section that shows funny stuff about
"Miss Your Cruising." You know, things like taking turns
sleeping on a cot while the other person stands watch, or
hanging by your knees upside down to change spark plugs
in your car.

But I gotta tell you, these are not the things I miss. Not
by a long shot. What I miss more than anything is the freedom to go somewhere. Anywhere! It doesn't matter. I just
feel so locked-in living on land. The place never moves! I
can't take it to Catalina for the weekend, or up the coast just
to anchor out off the beach for an evening.

It can drive you crazy. Of course, that's not a real long
trip for me, but the longer we are off the boat, the more I
miss just taking off for a sail.

Over the years I find that I go out a lot less for daysails.
After returning from a voyage of 10,000 miles, it sometimes
seems a little silly just to go out for a few hours. When you
are cruising, if you don't plan on having the sails up for

more than a few hours, you hardly bother putting them up. If it's only six or seven miles to the next anchorage, we find ourselves motoring. Not because we don't enjoy being under sail. That's not it. It's just that, when you run your motor you are "filling the bank." You know, charging the batteries, running the refer, maybe making water. When you cruise you have to do those things, and usually either your engine or a genset are what makes it happen.

Oh, don't get me wrong. The feeling I get when casting off to sail over to the local cruising grounds is still pretty much the same feeling I had 30 years ago. Each time I depart I know that something exciting will probably happen between the time we cast off and when we return and tie up. But since we have been unable to take the boat out of the slip, the old desire just to go out for an hour is coming back, and it is coming on stronger every day.

If you didn't think I was a little odd before this, then what I'm about to tell you should pretty much take care of it. You see, we just had a few days of torrential downpour. You know what I missed? The leaks!

Really! For so many years, a good downpour was what it would take to find out where the latest leaks were. All boaters know that leaks like to try and confuse us. One time it'll leak by the galley, and the next rain that area's dry and the leak has moved to the forward anchor locker. When we would get a torrential downpour I could wander through the boat, looking for telltale water, and then, when the weather cleared I knew where to look so I could fix them. We'd go for eight or nine months without any rain (it never rains in Southern California, or so the song says!) and when it would hit we'd find new places where the water had found its way through the paint, wood, fiberglass and epoxy that make up a boat.

This would usually point out a larger problem, which, if it hadn't rained, we wouldn't even know existed.

No, I'm not crazy enough to like problems (at least not yet!), but finding a problem that needs fixing is the first step to having it fixed, so it does add a little silver lining to the cloud cover.

It just seems like we are biding our time waiting until the boat's our home again. On the days when it is nice out we see our friends sailing by, heading out to the islands or up the coast, and we feel as if we are missing something. And we are. We miss our life.

Which kinda brought a weird image to my alleged mind. If I weren't a "sailor," just who the hell would I be? I look at myself standing on the dock, watching others take off for a daysail, or for a weekend anchored out, or even on a voyage of adventure, and I wonder how people who don't sail see this world we live on.

For me, when I see a satellite photo of the earth, I see untold adventures looking at the vast expanse of blue with scattered hard spots that we have sailed to. It warms the heart just looking at a globe. Can you imagine what it's like for people who don't sail? What do they see? A big blue ball, where they are restricted to live in little strips of land that are spotted around it?

I think the truth is, sailors have more fun than people!

You know you're a cruiser

The first time I sailed across an ocean as skipper was about 22 years ago. Prior to that I'd sailed up and down my coast. In the previous 10 years I was what you might call a coastal cruiser.

You know, a day sail to Catalina, an overnighter down to Mexico, things like that. Even the cruise I took down to Guatemala on the STONE WITCH was pretty much a coastal cruise. The farthest offshore we went was when we crossed the Sea of Cortez, and that was just a two-day sail.

During those formative years I studied cruising as if it were a course in school. I digested everything written by Lin and Larry, by Herb Payson, and of course, my personal hero, Earl Hinz.

What I'd gleaned from these books, as well as the magazines dedicated to cruising the world was that in order to be a true cruiser, you had to pretty well cut the ties behind you and go.

So it was pretty obvious to me that was the way to do it. Since I had to work for a living (kinda!) I was, by definition, a coastal cruiser. I would sail for a couple of days when I'd get a chance, and then return to make a buck or two in order to do it again.

Then one day I thought I had a plan. Even though I couldn't do it the right way, I could sail to Hawaii in a matter of three weeks or so, and then fly back to take care of business. Back then it wasn't unusual to find a $99 airfare from California to Hawaii, so it was feasible.

I was still a little dubious as to whether this was really considered cruising. After all, I wasn't selling the family farm, nor was I selling all my belongings and converting them to gold and storing it in my bilge. I felt as if I were cheating.

So it was that I convinced my friend Bruce to take a month off to come sail with me. I also convinced the girl I was dating at the time to quit her job and come sailing with us. This she did, and even convinced an old girlfriend of hers from Minnesota to join us.

We were off!

We took a little shakedown sail down the coast of Mexico to Cabo San Lucas, and after spending New Year's Eve in Cabo (now that is a truly daunting experience!) we took off at dawn on January 1.

As the sail progressed we felt like pioneers. Like we were the first people ever to try this venture. We relied on our sextant, as the GPS was about ten years in the future, and even satellite navigation systems were way out of our price range.

The day we spotted the Big Island of Hawaii was one of the highlights of my entire life. The feeling of accomplishment swelled until I thought I'd burst. I must've looked like a large, tattooed Cheshire Cat as we approached the islands.

I felt that I had accomplished something, but I still didn't feel that I was a real cruiser. That was reserved for those who cut the cord and didn't leave anything behind. Those were the real cruisers.

And so, for the next 10 years I cruised whenever possible, crossing the Pacific six times and sailing into Mexico and Central America about the same. But I wasn't a cruiser, or so I thought. Not yet.

Then I sold my business, sold pretty much everything I had, kidnapped Jody and sailed off into the sunset. At last I was a real cruiser.

And then, ten years later, I returned from the voyage. Returned to where? To what?

And then I realized the fallacy of my original dreams. Cruising is a state of mind, it's not a particular way of doing things. It's a way of how you look at things.

Sue Morgan, our editor, has lived aboard her Cheoy Lee 35-foot yawl with her husband, Mike, for 23 years. The vast majority of that time has been tied up in a slip, but they are cruisers. There's no doubt about it.

On the other hand, there are people I've met who did a circumnavigation and sold their boats never to sail again. These were not cruisers, they were adventurers. There's a big difference.

It's kinda like Richard Branson who just set a new speed record by sailing around the world. He's an adventurer, not a sailor. Next he will be in a balloon or a jet plane, trying to set more records.

Cruisers are a breed. They get excited when a movie like *Pirates of the Caribbean* comes out. In their spare time they get a joy out of looking at old charts, or planning a new voyage.

If you get a smile on your face when you see a sail on the horizon; if you grin whenever you're behind the wheel in a gale, you're a cruiser!

Reaping the rewards

*L*ife didn't get much better. We were about three hundred miles from entering the Mediterranean Sea. As
this would be the first time I sailed into this legendary
birthplace of sailing, I was about as giddy as a teenage boy
on his first date with Britney Spears.

We'd sailed directly from Antigua to the Azores, and
the trip had been made wearing shorts almost the whole
way.

Then we got hit by a blow in Horta and had to hole up
for about a week. We decided to head out a little before the
other boats, as the blow was subsiding.

We left the Azores in some pretty lofty company. Tom,
the skipper of the ketch TICONDEROGA, decided to leave at
the same time, so we were racing across the channel to
Gibraltar. I guess racing isn't exactly the right word. As we
left the islands, all we saw was his stern as it disappeared
over the horizon. But still, it was a good feeling to sail with
such a true classic yacht.

Yeah, I couldn't have been more content. We'd lost
sight of TICONDEROGA a couple days earlier, and now we
were just dreaming of the adventures that were to come
when we entered this new (to us) cruising playground.

Of course, as we all well know, God has a sense of
humor. On this particular day I figure She was feeling particularly peevish.

We'd been sailing at a fair clip with the wind about 120° off our stern. All of a sudden the wind shifted in a gust a little past the 180° mark. The mainsail shifted a little, and all of a sudden the boom was doing a jibe.

I hollered "jibe" at no one in particular, and ducked. Even though our mast is eight feet off the deck, it is still an eerie feeling having a few hundred pounds of aluminum swishing over your head.

And then I watched as, in slow motion (why do bad things always happen in slow motion?) the sheet line dipped down from the boom, grabbed the cute little mushroom thingy that sat atop our pilothouse, and popped it into the sea like a giant kicking a toadstool.

That cute little mushroom was our GPS antenna.

Oh joy! No GPS.

As the rest of the crew appeared on deck, I automatically started the man-overboard drill we had practiced so many times. I swung the bow into the wind, pulled the headsail in, eased the main sheet and started the motor. We slowly motored toward the white bobbing object in front of us, as Woody hung over the side to capture it as we pulled alongside.

After it was on board we realized just how little we knew about antennas and things. We opened it up, rinsed it with fresh water, and dried it in the sun. When we reconnected it there was no joy in Mudville. The GPS just blinked at us like my VCR used to do.

But, hey, we are world sailors. We know what to do, right? We have our backup. Our trusty Magnavox 4102 satellite receiver. I think every boat sailed in the 80s had one of those, and we had never taken ours off the boat!

(A brief note here. This happened in 1995, before backup handheld GPS were so inexpensive and available.)

We turned it on hopefully, and watched as it started to blink at us just like the GPS. I think they were related.

It soon hit me that, in the old days you had to put your position into the thing to get it started. We didn't know our position.

So, out comes our handy-dandy sextant.

To make a long story short, the 10 years since I'd taken a sight had melted the old memory a bit. It was well after noon the next day when we got our position, as all I could remember was how to take a noon sight (hey, it had been 10 years!).

We set the Sat/Nav, and soon all was well with the world again.

I remember the feeling I had as we entered the Strait of Gibraltar and I first sighted that venerable rock. I also realized that that feeling came not only from entering a new cruising ground, but more from the fact that we had faced a challenge and solved it.

In the world we live in, we are so protected it is very seldom we can achieve the feeling of self-worth that can only be found after conquering a difficult situation. One where, even for a split second, you feel the hairs on the back of your neck stand up.

And that, my friend, is why we go out there. For that split second when you can feel you are reaping the rewards of your labors. You have to slay the dragon before you can kiss the princess!

X-Y chromosome

We've all heard about the X chromosome and the Y chromosome. These little invisible thingies that were launched in our collective DNA at birth make some of us want to shop and others like football. There's nothing one can do about these pre-selected idiosyncrasies, so you might as well just enjoy wearing pink or wearing blue.

So what's this got to do with cruising? Well, here's the deal. I think that there is also a C chromosome. C for Cruising. Not only do I believe it, but I think I can prove it. So kick back for a second and follow along as I try to explain my point.

Fact 1: There are some folks we will call Control Group C. They love to go out to sea in small plastic bathtub-looking thingies, tie a bed-sheet to a stick and go back and forth or in large circles. They call this sailing, and they do this on purpose, for fun.

Fact 2: The vast majority of people on this earth—we shall designate these folks as Control Group NC—go their whole lives without ever setting foot on one of these sail-boats.

Fact 3: When there is interaction between Group C and Group NC, there is much consternation in both groups as one tries to explain to the other just how insane they really are.

Fact 4: At the end of such a discussion, each group

walks away shaking their collective heads saying, "They just don't get it."

This, my friends, is what is known as a paradox.

Paradox is heretowith explained as: par•a•dox n = a statement of proposition, or situation that seems to be absurd or contradictory, but in fact, is or may be true.

It is known there is a group of people out there with an exceptionally large amount of the C chromosome who actually go to sleep at night picturing themselves being out at sea on a boat as the sun is setting, thousands of miles from land. They have a smile on their face, and they sleep like babies with this picture deeply imprinted on their alleged minds.

At the same time, as near as the person sleeping next to them, is someone who was unfortunate enough not to get much of this C chromosome. With exactly the same picture imprinted on their mind, they are having a nightmare.

Same scene, but one lives to make it come true, and another would rather live in Death Valley than experience such a thing.

And therein, my friend, lies the salvaging of our dream.

Imagine, if you will, the utter turmoil and disruption of our lives if everybody out there felt as we did. Let's say that a new super drug is invented that makes you live to 133 years of age, but the side effect is you get a double dose of C.

At first it would be bliss! All of a sudden, those rules restricting liveaboards would be dropped, as there wouldn't be all those people against our lifestyle.

The boat brokers would all be happy, their offices would be palaces, and the highest paid profession on earth would be yacht broker.

General Electric and Boeing would be rebuilding their production lines, and cruising yachts would drop in price as the production became more automated. Those who build the boats would have phenomenal business growth, and the shipwright would be as envied a position as the dot.commers were a couple years back.

As more people got into the industry, there would be great strides in off-the-grid power supplies. Solar and wind generators would have whole scientific communities working on how to make them more efficient.

But, there'd be a downside. Yacht club memberships would start to cost more than golf club memberships. Marinas would be filled to overflowing, and the waters would be overcrowded with new boats.

In a matter of a year or two, the quiet backwaters of Suverov Island and the Great Barrier Reef would be featuring Dock-o-miniums!

The new world power would be the country of Kiribati! Bora Bora would be the new financial center of the world.

So, perhaps we should secretly say thanks to the God of creation who saw fit to only infuse the very brightest of individuals with sufficient C chromosomes to know just how precious a sunset on the equator really is. Perhaps aquaphobia is not such a bad thing for the other guy to have.

The barroom advice

So, you're sitting in a waterfront bistro after a great day's sail, downing your favorite libation and loving life, when you happen to hear the conversation at the next table. A young couple are discussing the beauty of sailing, and talking about the boats they had looked at that day.

Being a helpful kind of person, you good-naturedly turn to them and offer your sage advice. After all, you're a sailor, and you know this kind of stuff. Why not cast forth this wisdom to those less fortunate?

So you chip in with, "Pardon me, but I couldn't help but overhear, you guys are looking for a sailboat?"

"Why yes, we are!" they excitedly reply. "We are looking for a cruising boat. Do you sail?"

You put on your sagest expression and answer to the affirmative, suggesting that perhaps they should consider your type of vessel.

Meanwhile, at the next table, another sailor is sitting and sipping his favorite libation. He also has overheard the conversation, and after seeing you jump in, he, of course, would like to add his two cents worth. After all, spreading knowledge is the basis for civilization, right?

However, it seems that you and he don't see eye to eye on the best type of sailing vessel.

He is the owner of a (monohull or multihull, insert your

favorite here) and you happen to prefer a (monohull or multihull, insert your favorite here).

Now, being a normal human-type being, you don't want to look stupid. If you were to allow these people to think the gentleman at table B has the right boat, that would then lead to the assumption that you have chosen the wrong type of boat. In other words, you are not so bright—also known as an idiot. Are you going to allow this person to call you an idiot?

Why, of course not! So you chime back in with, "Oh yeah, well, my (monohull or multihull, insert your favorite here) is a better boat than your (monohull or multihull, insert your favorite here).

My friend, you have just jammed your size thirteen up well past the knee joint into your pie hole!

You see, as you are well aware, a boat purchase is one of the largest you will make in your lifetime. One must assume that you have given grave and serious consideration to all the options, and when you did choose, you chose the best type vessel available.

Of course, the gentleman at table B went through the very same torment when buying his boat, and he feels equally as strong about being right.

Let's jump ahead about a half hour. You are now standing face to face with the gentleman at table B in the middle of the bar, and patrons are all staring at the two red-faced dunderheads hollering about how one's (monohull or multihull, insert your favorite here) is better than the other's (monohull or multihull, insert your favorite here).

The young couple gave up a few minutes ago. They have opted to take up kayaking and have headed out to buy a good pair of Cobra kayaks.

Face it. This is a no-win situation. If there was only one right kind of boat there would be only one boat being made. We wouldn't need to think about it.

As the harbor police arrive to drag off the two grown men who are red-faced and rolling on the floor shouting obscenities at each other while trying to beat each other into submission, a young couple glides by the patrol boat on their brand new kayaks.

"Look Martha, isn't that the two nice men who were telling us about their boats?" the young man asks, as they pass the (monohull or multihull, insert your favorite here) that would have changed their life, if only you'd not offered your advice.

The moral to this story?

There is none. Now let's go sailing!

Wrong Bay Bob

————————▶◀————————

Wrong Bay Bob. That is what they are calling me (I get no respect!) after a little mishap on the New Zealand Share the Sail. Yes folks, I did it. I screwed up!

Oh, it's not like this is the first time I have done so. Oh no, I am a pretty frequent screwup. If they gave frequent screwup mileage, I'd be flying for free in first class all the time. No, that's not what I am getting at. The thing that was bad about this was, I didn't realize it until well after my mistake had been discovered by a whole bunch of people, and now I have to smile each time the story is retold.

Just so you know what I'm talking about, I shall simplify your life by giving a short recap here. We were sailing a three-boat flotilla out of Opua in the Bay of Islands, and it was raining so hard you couldn't see the bow of the boat. I was the lead boat, with Captain Woody and Tania following. The boats we were on didn't have GPS, radar or chartplotters, but I've been sailing for about 30 years and learned on a square-rigger that was similarly equipped. I trusted my senses.

In order to find our way into a good anchorage, I had to keep ducking below where the chart could be kept dry, and then coming up and trying to match landmarks with islands on the chart. As we passed a small island, the downpour increased to where there was very little vision. I was looking for a headland that I was planning to duck behind. I saw a dark shape looming in the downpour and headed for it. It seemed to be in the right direction. Having sailed for so many years, you get a sense of direction that very seldom lets you down. Even in a downpour, with dark clouds and blowing wind, I was sure I knew right where I was heading.

I went the wrong way!

The next day, when the sun had come out and things could be seen, I was asked where we were. I pointed confidently to a bay on the chart and said, "Right here!" I was very secure in my mind that that was where we were. The contour of the bay was real close, and the depths were only slightly off, which I attributed to unfamiliar gauges.

When it was discovered that we were about a quarter mile away from the actual bay I thought I was in, I still didn't want to admit I was wrong. I was sure, from the sense of direction that had never let me down before, that I was right, even though all the facts pointed to my error.

A little later that day, after a thorough razzing by everybody on our voyage, plus all the cruisers anchored nearby, I was talking with Tom Brownell, a friend who was on the cruise with me. Tom has been sailing all of his life and is a third generation boat builder out of Mattapoisett in Buzzards Bay, Massachusetts. He had the same feeling.

I was sitting, looking at the compass, and saw we were facing north. My inner direction finder was telling me I was facing south. I asked Tom to point to the north. Unhesitatingly, he pointed to the south. I pointed at the compass. We both felt so strongly about it we wanted to argue with the compass.

And then it hit us simultaneously. For the past ten years we had both been sailing in the northern hemisphere.

Without even thinking about it, our minds were using the fact that, in the north, you get warmer going south. No matter what time of day, even in a blinding rainstorm, there is always a little more light to the south, and that is what your brain bases your sense of direction on.

In the southern hemisphere, it's brighter to the north. The moss grows on the southern side of the trees, so to speak.

Now, I have sailed the southern hemisphere before, but it was always on my own boat after sailing across the equator, and I was able to "adjust" my inner compass over a period of time. Flying down in an aluminum box at night, there was no adjusting my sense over time.

For the rest of our voyage down under, Tom and I had to look at the charts upside down. It just "didn't feel right" when we'd turn them right side up. We were down there three weeks, and the feeling never changed.

The moral of this story? Hell, there is none. I guess I was just trying to justify my unwanted new nickname, "Wrong Bay Bob."

Ready to go?

Did you ever notice how the closer to taking off on a voyage you get, the more you start worrying about things that you know you can't do anything about? I am specifically thinking back on my departure early last year on a little 2,700-mile voyage across the Pacific. Joining Jody and me on this trek were three people I had not sailed with before, and an old friend who had sailed with us in the past.

Now I have always had a kind of rule I try to go by. If you are going on a voyage, the hardest thing to do is to set the departure date, so just set the damn thing and then make everything happen according to that schedule. In the last years, I have always tried to stick to this rule.

So, the date was fast approaching for our departure. Our inexperienced but enthusiastic crew arrived the day before D-Day, just in time for our going away party. After all, how can you miss me if I don't go away?

So, the night of our party the heavens opened up, and we had biblical amounts of cold and wet stuff falling on our heads. The winds were blowing harder than a politician on election night. It was not a pretty sight, and the weather guys were saying it would get worse before it got any better, and that would be days later. Pretty much, this was the biggest storm we'd seen in over a year.

Did I care? Not in the least! As a matter of fact, I was

kinda looking forward to leaving in a storm. What a great feeling; to set sail with a double reef, heading out the harbor entrance, leaving mouths agape! How kewl!

But I have to tell you, my erstwhile crew were not quite of the same mind set. Actually, they thought I'd lost mine. My mind, that is.

Having made numerous departures in the past, I knew that what we were experiencing sitting here in the harbor was in no way as bad as what we were likely to encounter out there. Of course, I had the good sense not to tell them that. I'd have to face down a mutiny if I'd told them my reasons.

But, believe it or not, I did have an alternative purpose to taking off that next morning, in a full gale. As a matter of fact, after I wrote the story of that voyage, I received a number of nasty letters telling me I was remiss in my duties as a magazine person to set such dangerous precedents; to put my crew in harm's way instead of sitting safe in the harbor until the storm blew by, and then taking off in good weather.

Hogwash and bullpuckie! That's pretty much my reply to that. You see, in the next three days my stalwart crew sailed through gale winds and 16-20 foot seas as we fought our way out of the harbor and down to Long Beach for fuel, and then 300 miles south, blown almost 20° off our preferred course. As we sailed, they learned that the boat could handle it, and to their surprise, so could they. They actually started to enjoy the adventure.

And then one morning the winds started to subside. As that day progressed, the seas started to slacken, and by midday of the fourth day at sea, the sun came out to warm us, and to dry our saturated vessel.

We, as a crew, had braved the worst that the seas could throw at us (or so it seemed!) and came through none the worse for wear. We had conquered the sea gods and could see things starting to improve and keep improving until, at last, we were sailing in what most people hope to find, perfect weather and a downwind sail.

Now let me ask you, if we had sat until the weather had cleared, and left in good weather, what would we have had to look forward to? Nothing but deteriorating weather and conditions ahead of us. As it was, we had conquered the bad stuff, knew we could handle it as a crew, and knew, without any doubt, it would get better . . .

Ponder this: is it better to be in good weather, looking ahead to darkening skies, and worry about what is to come; or to sit under that dark cloud, looking forward to the brightening sky and know you have seen the bad, and know you are about to enter Nirvana?

It is best said in the old adage, Give me the strength to change the things that I can, the serenity to live with the things that I can't, and the wisdom to know the difference. And perhaps we should add a tag line to that verse: . . . and the option to choose the order in which I face these things!

The third day

There is this phenomenon in sailing that happens on just about your third day of an ocean crossing. The evening of day two you will usually be sitting, looking back at where land used to be, wondering just what the heck you were thinking when you decided to come out here in the first place. The boat's rocking has become annoying, the meals are hard to fix, and the weather is cold and windy. You really start to have doubts about your sanity!

And then comes day three!

It is in about the third day when you enter "Cruise Mode."

Cruise Mode is a state of mind not dissimilar to hibernation. All of a sudden everything goes into its own time zone. The days actually seem to get a lot shorter. It is about here in a voyage where you start to adapt to the time schedule of a cruising vessel. You know, watch schedules, meals, stuff like that. It all starts to go into automation.

On the dawn of the third day you are usually thinking, "What the heck was I thinking? It's only been two days and we got another two weeks until we get back to land! Am I nuts?"

Then you awaken on day four. Magic has occurred! You sit up on your bunk, and all of a sudden the annoying rocking and rolling has turned into a comforting sway. You don't even notice how your body adjusts to the swells and the heel of the boat. It seems natural.

You grab a cup out of the cupboard and pour a cup of coffee. The day before you spilled it because the %^$%$#!! boat wouldn't stop moving! Now you just swing the cup to match the motion. You don't even notice you are doing it.

As you leave the cabin and walk topside you hear a cheerful voice, "Good morning, sleep well?" The person on watch is glad to see you, because now they have someone to talk to after a few hours alone with their thoughts, enjoying the dawn.

After a while you grab your book and stuff a beanbag chair against the mast, making a comfortable nest, and drop your body into it. Soon you are lost in the world of literature. Occasionally you'll look over the top of your book, and just stare out across the blue water, letting your mind drift to a hundred pasts and a hundred planned futures.

Your reverie will then be broken by someone asking you if you're hungry. It'll take a few seconds for you to figure if it is supposed to be breakfast, lunch or dinner. Remembering it's breakfast, you walk back to the cockpit, and enjoy the company of your crewmates, and some easy-to-prepare meal.

Soon, you'll find yourself back in the beanbag, probably checking your eyelids for holes (sleeping!) when it's time for your watch. After a while you start looking forward to the watch. Little rivalries develop, like seeing who will cover the most water during their watch, or what wildlife will be spotted. Whales, dolphins or sea birds, and of course, the real prize, when a fish is caught!

The days start to run together. Trying to remember

when something happened on a crossing becomes a real game. Actually, trying to remember what day it is becomes tough. You know you are lost in Cruise Mode when you can't remember what month it is. Then you have entered Nirvana, a true cruising paradise.

By the end of a crossing you can't recall over half the days behind you. They just seem to run together. On one crossing to Hawaii, as we entered Hawaiian waters we didn't want to stop. We kept sailing for another 120 miles, past The Big Island, past the beautiful island of Maui and its old whaling capital, Lahaina, and on into the channel between Maui and Molokai.

We sailed past the old wreck on the coast of the island of Lanai, and felt the pull of the trades as we entered the Molokai channel.

Sailing on a downwind broad reach, we watched huge humpback whales jumping out of the water with what only can be pure joy of living. We wanted to do the same.

The truth of the matter is, you have to experience a little bit of hell to truly enjoy the bountiful gift of heaven. The trials and tribulations of a long voyage are directly balanced on the end of that voyage by the feeling of accomplishment that fills you.

You put the last sail tie on, pull the sail covers in place, and pull into the harbor that signifies the completion of your voyage. It is here that you will understand why sailors, for thousands of years, have left safe harbors and challenged the sea!

Saltwater cures all

————————►◄————————

We were about 50 miles out of Palmyra Island, on the 900+ mile voyage to Hawaii. There was Jody and I, and two young crewmembers we'd had with us since Papeete, almost three months, Luke and Joel.

All of a sudden the boat started to swerve off course.

I figured it was the 15-year-old autopilot acting up, so I turned it off and grabbed the wheel, giving it a turn. It turned to full lock and nothing happened. We were going in circles.

So here we were, 850 miles from civilization, and 50 miles from a semi-deserted island. I went below and lifted the aft bunk. There was the problem. Our steering gudgeon had broken in half. Without it, we couldn't steer the boat.

There was no panic. No running around wringing our hands with worry. Just a couple of minutes trying to remember where we put the emergency tiller three years earlier, when we left our homeport.

Remembering where it was, we dug it out from under a bunch of stores and spares. It was an eight-foot stainless thingamabob that looked like a socket extension, with a swiveling bar on the top. We unscrewed the emergency tiller access plate and stuck the thing down into the black hole, wiggling it until it dropped onto the top of the rudder post. Kewl. It fit.

I dropped the tiller bar into place, checked the bolt to

●●

make sure it was tight and secure, and gave it a tender push to test the rudder.

It snapped off in my hand.

Oh joy!

The fifteen years it had sat unused had weakened the weld, and all it took was a little pressure to snap it off. Now what?

After thinking for a couple of minutes, I sent Luke down to the tool bin and had him bring up two of the large pipe wrenches that we keep on board to tighten the packing gland. We placed them facing each other on the emergency rudder pole, and wrapped them with a small piece of line. When finished we had a small tiller post.

Now here we were, in the middle of nowhere, with a broken rudder, and just a 12- to 15-inch tiller handle to steer a 42-ton ship. If I were reading this I would be really worried. Thinking about it, it seems like we would have been in a real fix, but I can recall with crystal clarity how I felt . . . excited!

Really! This was what world cruising is all about. Getting into situations that allow you to use your God-given sense to overcome adversity, and feel the surge of adrenaline when you first know you have done it.

For the next ten hours we motored back towards Palmyra. We had to steer by bracing our backs against the rail and pushing with all our might with our legs. It took two people on the rudder at all times. I was very thankful to have Luke and Joel with us. Their 19-year-old legs worked better (and longer) than my 50-year-old variety.

As Palmyra came into view the next morning, the people on the two boats inside came out to help us through the pass, along with Roger, the island caretaker.

We had made it. There is no way on earth for a person to feel the exhilaration of conquest without first having to overcome adversity. The harder fought the battle, the more heartfelt the victory.

And that is why we go to sea. No one wants anything to go wrong. We don't plan on having things break, or storms hit us; but we know, sometimes between the time we leave our homeport and the time we return, something will happen that we will remember for the rest of our lives. A moment in time when you will have the same feeling David had when Goliath hit the dirt. The same feeling Columbus felt when he sighted San Salvador.

And the same feeling I had when we sighted Palmyra Island, that beautiful day in 1993.

Whenever I think about Luke or Joel, who have gone on to college, and to their lives, I think back on that night, laughing through the pain of overworked and cramping legs. Taking turns at doing the impossible, and feeling the release as our goal came into view.

There is an old saying that saltwater cures all ills: sweat, tears or the sea. When all three combine, when the ills become an ordeal, and are overcome, that's an adventure!

The two happiest days

I am referring to the old saying, "The two happiest days in a sailor's life are the day he buys his boat, and the day he sells it." This is usually accompanied by a knowing wink, and told to a man who has just bought his dream boat, only to find out that the portholes were an added cost option.

Actually these are not the happiest days in a sailor's life. Not by a long shot. I think one of the two happiest days in a sailor's life has to be the day he actually drops the dock lines at his home marina, and sets sail on a voyage that has been planned for years.

To accomplish one's dream has to be a pretty intense rush. Accompany that with the stomach-churning adrenaline rush of actually waving to those on shore, and departing on a journey that you know will test your very being, adds a little cream to the filling. Then add the knowledge that, before you return to that dock, you will live adventures that others only dream about.

I don't think I will ever forget the morning I left Redondo Beach on the topsail schooner STONE WITCH, bound for Guatemala. It was my first extended sailing adventure, over 20 years ago. Alan Olsen, the owner, wanted to make the trip, but didn't have the money to go. I had the money to go, but didn't have the boat, or the experience, so we joined forces.

I don't think I will ever forget the feeling, that very first morning, as we hoisted the hook (by hand, there was no windlass, or engine for that matter!). I looked back at the marina I had lived in for the past couple years, and I think I actually felt my heart swell with pride. I had done it. Set off on an adventure that I knew would change my life.

Two hours later I was puking over the side, seasick as any landlubber, as we were becalmed less than two miles off the harbor entrance.

Believe it or not, I look back on that day as one of the best days of my life. It took a couple of days for my system to adjust to being at sea full time. Until then I had only day sailed for a few hours at a time. But it passed. The sickness. Not the feeling.

But that was not the very best day I have ever had. Close, but still it stands as number two.

No, number one was reserved for the first time I actually captained my first voyage across a major ocean, and made landfall. Back then we didn't have GPS, and Sat/Nav was way too expensive. I used a sextant. Roller furling was pretty new, and not many cruisers were using it yet, so we used our hands to haul and hank-on sails. Weatherfax? A dream for most cruisers.

That was part of the beauty of the day. We had fought bad weather, used our hands and muscles, our basic intelligence, and a little old fashioned adventuring spirit, and landed in Hawaii just as Captain Cook had done a few hundred years before us. What a feeling!

Over the past years I have bought and sold a number of boats. Okay, I have to admit, the feeling of unloading a cash-hole and standing there with a wad of green can make you smile, but it is always accompanied by the feeling that you have just let go of a friend. It's bittersweet at best.

And the day you buy a boat? Let me ask you this, as most of you are boat owners. Can you recall how you felt the day you bought your boat? Let's see. A whole bunch of anxiety, like "Was this the best boat for me?" or, "Could I have gotten a better deal?" or better yet, "Maybe I should have gotten a bigger/smaller (make your own selection) boat!"

No, I think I am going to drop that old wives' tale from my repertory. I know for a fact that the best two days of a man's life are not the days that he buys and/or sells a boat, unless, of course, you happen to be a yacht broker. . . . then it could be true I guess.

But if there is one truth about happiness you can glean from all this excess verbiage, it is the fact that the best two days of one's life can indubitably be found somewhere in between the day you buy a boat, and the day you sell it.

So let's get out there and see if we can find those days!

Finding a way

Why is it our whole life seems to change just because we have untied a couple of silly knots and cast off to go on a cruise? I mean, did you ever notice how you actually enjoy fixing stuff that breaks when you're anchored in a strange anchorage? Let the same light switch go awry in your homeport, and it's a pain in the derriere to fix it!

I remember fighting to make it into Niuatoputapu in Tonga with a 3-inch hole in an exhaust elbow doing its best to sink the LOST SOUL. We discovered this annoying little hole when it was about a quarter of an inch, and ol' Poop-fer-Brains (that's me!) figures the best way to see how bad it is would be to press on the metal that was still holding. Voilà! A three-inch hole from a quarter-inch hole in just a matter of milliseconds! Kewl, huh!

So there we were, 10 miles from land, with a river running through our bilge, our bilge pumps doing their best to keep the boat afloat, and I'm having the time of my life.

Excitement! It's the spice to life's meat! Nothing makes a person feel more alive than conquering adversity. Figuring what it's gonna take to get safely into port, and then fixing the problem that caused the hassle. Each is an element in helping keep your inner juices flowing.

Oh, don't get me wrong, I'm not suggesting you go around breaking stuff or causing problems just so you can fix them. I'm not that sick! All I am saying is, highs and lows are better than static. Of course you already know that, because that's what drives most of us out to sea.

But, then I think back on when we pulled into the small northern Tongan island's lagoon. The feeling of accomplishment for overcoming the adversity was overwhelming. It was a natural high that is unequaled.

Even after we'd turned ourselves black with oil and exhaust-based grunge, pulling the offending part out, we were still feeling it.

And then there was the real dessert to our feeding frenzy of feelings. Finding a way to Mickey Mouse (sorry Walt!) a way to fix a hole in a three-inch galvanized exhaust elbow on an island where bamboo pipes are considered high-tech. Paradise!

Even sitting here, three years later, I can remember the way everyone on board chimed in with ideas. What in a homeport would have been a miserable and grungy job, was actually an adventure for us all.

Once the hole in the elbow had been repaired we all stood back and looked at our masterpiece with a pride only a parent can feel with a gifted child. It was stronger than new and extremely functional! A real Rube Goldberg! You couldn't help but laugh when you'd look at it. A galvanized piece of pipe wrapped with a beer can, bonded in West epoxy, duct tape and wire. But, it worked!

For the next three months, and 2,500 miles, whenever anyone on the boat started to get a little grumpy or come down with a case of "Bad Attitude," we'd just march the offending crewmember down to the engine room, and make them look at our fixit. If that didn't get a smile on the lips and a chuckle in the throat they were doomed to be grumpy for life.

Even after we'd sailed into Pago Pago and bought a new elbow, we kept our little fixit job in place, figuring we'd replace it when it started to leak. It never did. It became a point of pride with all who sailed on the LOST SOUL. We left it in place until almost a year later when we arrived back in our homeport, and rebuilt the whole system.

We all learned from that elbow. As silly as it seems, whenever I start to lose my starboard attitude, I can usually find it again. All I have to do is think back to Niuatoputapu, and how a bunch of grown people stood around gloping epoxy and tape and wire around a little piece of pipe, and how good it made us feel to accomplish something as menial and trivial as that.

And the beauty of cruising is, I know that ahead of me, somewhere, is a time and place when I will, once again, get to fight the dragons of adversity, and come out on top with some silly idea.

And that, my friend, is what makes life worth living.

Think you're smart?

*H*ave you ever noticed how there is only one right opinion, and that is yours? You know, only one right way to do things. One correct anchoring method, one way to sail from one point to the next?

Probably one of the things that cruisers enjoy about sitting in an anchorage as it fills with boats at the end of the day is watching how dumb all other boaters are. Come on, we've all done it.

"Hey, check out how this guys' anchoring. Bet he drags."

"Look at that headsail, must be a new sailor."

"Why would anyone anchor over there? This is a much better spot."

What I always equate it to is driving down a freeway. When someone is going slower than you it's, "Hey, what an idiot, why doesn't he go faster!"

Then you get passed by a speeding vehicle and it's all about, "Yo, is that guy crazy, look how fast he's going!"

Yup, the only people who are right are those who are going the same speed as you, unless of course you are having a really bad day, and then it's all about, "What's up with this guy, he's pacing me."

It's almost humorous out in the anchorages. If you belong to the school that says to lay out six-to-one scope, and you see a boater come in and drop a hundred feet of chain in 25 feet of water, and, whoa, this guy must be nuts. But a week later you could be coming into the same anchorage and, knowing the area, drop the same hundred feet, knowing you are just staying for an hour or so.

Sure, there are books and books and hundreds of articles telling you just how everything should be done, but, in the end, each skipper is responsible for his own vessel, and isn't that what makes cruising such a fulfilling way of life?

If there was only one right way to do things there would only be one design of boat, one anchor design and one type of engine. In reality it just isn't so. There are more right ways and wrong ways to do things than anyone could imagine. The only thing that gets us to the correct answer for us is experience.

You can read a dozen books by the authorities about how to anchor in every and all situations, but until you have actually dropped a hook, it's all theory. The more times you drop a hook, the more variations you will learn. It's easy. It's also the fun part. The learning.

Experienced cruisers are always being asked by the new sailor for tips about how to make things easier. Being told how to lay an anchor chain in a big blow is one thing, but after you have done it, well, you just never forget. As your cruising experiences mount up, your cruising knowledge builds.

How can you get this knowledge before you go cruising?

Ah, there is the rub. What comes first, the chicken or the egg? The knowledge to cruise, or the cruise?

There is nothing worse than packing up all your belongings and heading out to sea, only to learn a week later that you hate the lifestyle.

What I did was to find a boat heading out, and offer to share some of the expenses in order to share some of the experiences. I found that I loved the lifestyle, returned home, bought the boat I felt was right for me, and here I sit with 100,000 miles behind me.

The difference? Simple. I don't know any more than I did then, but people think I do, so it's okay. Now when I pull in and drop a hook people say, "He must know what he's doing, because he's cruised the world!" Whereas, in reality, I still do stuff as stupid as I did 25 years ago. Only now people think I do it on purpose!

A couple of weeks ago Jody and I escaped to a little anchorage to get away from it all, and I backed right onto a pile of rocks (which was well marked on the charts, by the way). All of a sudden I remembered that, 25 years ago, on my first trip to that bay, I had backed onto the same pile of rocks.

All of a sudden I thought back to that far off day, and a chill came over me, because I could remember so vividly how scared I was when I'd done it that first time. And I also remembered how horrendously stupid I felt, thinking that it was because I was so new to sailing, and that, with time at sea and a little experience, I wouldn't do stupid stuff like that anymore. I would learn!

And here I sat, 25 years and a dozen oceans behind me, on the same stupid pile of rocks, with the same silly feeling in my gut, and I still believe that someday I will have the experience needed to avoid such things.

Across the bay I saw a boater watching me, and chuckling.

Life is maintenance
➤◄━━━━━━━━

I was sitting with my legs wrapped around a toilet bowl, and I was laughing out loud. All of a sudden it seemed funny. A bit earlier I was about to toss the darn thing over the side in silent rage. Then it hit me. Something my tormentor used to say when I'd bitch about having to fix one of the many things that would break on a daily basis on my boat.

"Hey man, life is maintenance," he'd grin, "so what's the problem?"

We were sailing off the coast of Nicaragua when the forward head went into the crapper (get it, head went into the crapper? Oh, never mind).

We had managed to get it off and to the forward deck where we could work on it in fresh air. Somewhere in the process of dismantling, rebuilding, and repairing it, a crucial screw decided to hide. You know how it is. The one screw you can't replace? We ended up re-tapping the part to use a screw we had (which we had to cut to fit in the first place) and finally got it to work.

Then, as I sat there contemplating the job that had taken two hours but should have taken 30 minutes, the errant screw came rolling out from under the cushion I was sitting on.

We've all heard the old saying that cruising is fixing your boat in exotic and beautiful locations, and that really is the truth. No matter how much time and money you put in your vessel, as soon as you leave your homeport something is going to stop working, and for the rest of your cruise, as with your life, things will need fixing.

As your cruise extends from months into years, you will find that most of the adventures you will have revolve around fixing something on your boat.

You'll be sitting on a beach in Bora-Bora, or at a taverna in Greece, talking with other cruisers. Most of the funny stories you'll be telling will be about how you had to find a gasket for your hydraulic steering ram in Pago Pago, or how you learned to substitute a ball point pen spring for a fuse spring in mid-Pacific.

The adventures you will relish will be the time you had to pay $80 for a one-foot piece of used exhaust hose in the south of France, or how you found replacement 12-volt fans for $5 while shopping at a gypsy's caravan in Crete.

One thing I found while cruising is that there are a lot of folks who actually enjoy the maintenance. If you were extremely active in your previous life, chances are you will want to remain so. Maintenance on your vessel is one way to keep puttering.

I remember once cruising with a small flotilla of about six boats on the upwind leg out of Panama up the Pacific coast of Central America. After crossing the Sea of Tehuantepec, we pulled into Acapulco. The first thing most of us wanted was to hit the bar and discuss the trip up over a large, cold cerveza.

Except for Mike Harbin on Aries II. He opted to stay aboard and clean his rigging and detail his engine room. The next day, when we finally got to sit down over a cold one together, he said it made him feel better knowing every-thing was shipshape.

It just depends on what's comfortable for you.

There are people who go to the extremes of painting all their teak brightwork so they won't have to varnish, and others who prefer to keep the varnish up, even though it takes a lot of work. The beauty of cruising is, both people are right. Everyone has a different agenda, and no one's is wrong, because once you are out there, you make your own rules. What's right for one person is not necessarily right for another.

And that carries right on through to the boat itself. There are those who opt to drink tepid Kool-Aid and sail sans engine, and there are those of us who prefer the clink of ice and the curse of refrigeration.

Who's right? Who knows? And more important, who the hell cares?

Let's go cruising.

PART 4

Living the Dream

Enjoy the moment

So, the other night we were at a marina bash, and as it usually turns out, all the guys are hanging around discussing important world events, like where's the best place to get a cheap beer when cruising Mexico, and all the ladies are up on the dance floor entertaining the troops.

As I sat there and looked around, I realized just what a great lifestyle we have happened upon. I mean, everywhere in the world people are worrying about where the next bomb will explode, and our biggest problem at the time was how to go get another cold beer without losing your seat in the round-table discussion.

I remember standing on "Y" dock almost 20 years ago, talking with my neighbor. He had a 42-foot sloop in the next slip, and we were discussing just how unfair life had treated him. He'd just sold his computer company for a few million dollars and the tax man had seen fit to charge him an extra million in taxes because he'd kept the property the building sat on.

As he sat there discussing the dubious parentage of the taxman and taxmen in general, a seal swam by us, popped to the surface and started flipping a fish he'd just caught up into the air and then catching it.

Our conversation stopped for a couple of minutes as we watched him frolic with his lunch, and as the seagulls came over to see if they couldn't score a few morsels as well.

As the gulls were screaming, "Mine! Mine! Mine!" (I loved that part in *Finding Nemo*), I looked over at him, and he had this big smile on his face.

"Ya know," he said, as he caught me looking at him, "I guess I'm being pretty stupid, huh?"

"Lemme see if I have this right," I asked. "Your biggest problem in life is that you just paid a million dollars in taxes?"

The reality of it is, no matter what your lifestyle, you'll get a lot further in being happy with your life if you stop trying to find out what it is that sucks and look at what makes it good.

An old friend of mine, Doug McLoud, who is a blues singer by vocation, put it about as well as I've ever heard it.

"You can spot people who aren't happy in life. They walk into a room looking like they smell something bad."

Think about it! It's like the guy that finds a $5 bill laying in the street and snivels because it wasn't a $20. You know people like that. We all do. The scary thing is, sometimes we all get into that kind of funk.

Stop for a minute and think about whatever it is that has been your major malfunction in the past few weeks. Something that has just bugged you and kept you tossing and turning in the still of the night. Put it mentally into a hat with other people's troubles, and see if you don't try and pull your own problem out of the hat.

Now roll this philosophy into our lifestyle of cruising. On my most recent sail across the Pacific a few months back, I found myself getting peeved at little things that would break: a stuck bilge switch, a light that burns out, a generator that won't start. Each time, my first reaction was to snivel to myself, "Why me . . . Why now?"

But you know what? Here we were, on a beautiful sailboat that I (and the bank!) own, sailing across the Pacific Ocean with friends. How could life have been any better?

Yeah, little things will always go wrong, and you'd have to be a nut (or a saint) for them not to bother you. But the next time something like that happens, take a step back and see just how bad it is in reality. Compare it to being born Helen Keller, and your troubles pale by comparison.

Everyone knows the old fable about the man who was sniveling about having no shoes, and then he met a man with no legs. Well, the next time your bilge pump breaks, remember, some of us have to use a manual pump!! Imagine!!

And so, as I sat there with a half dozen people who live my lifestyle, I felt warm inside. They were laughing and joking about the little things that happen with boats, and all was well with the world. We would worry about terrorism and work another day. This was the time we were meant to enjoy. And we did.

Today, I sit here looking back on that yesterday, and I count it as a keeper. A "keeper" is a certain amount of time that, somehow, will pop up throughout my life.

As long as you get enough keepers, what happens the rest of the time is irrelevant.

Every moment you really enjoy in your life is worth whatever time it took to make it happen.

Living the dream

▶◀

When I was first getting into the sailing life, I heard about a book called *An Island to Oneself* written by a man named Tom Neale. He was a New Zealander who had a dream. That dream became an obsession—to find the perfect island and be the only man to live on that island.

Over the years, my obsession with cruising pretty well matched what I imagined his fervor to be.

I say imagine, because I didn't read the book.

No, I got a copy of it, but I didn't read it. I had this idea that the best place to read the book would be on the island that the book was written about.

Oh, I remember articles written about the man. Stories of how he lived as a hermit on the island of Suverov (aka Suwarrow), a small speck that I located on a map of the world, and it was about the size of a fly speck, dead in the center of the South Pacific.

I read how cruisers would stop by his island to visit. He would have them sign his guest book and he would visit with them, sometimes one or two a year, and one year as many as six. I read in various cruising magazines how he'd become ill. How a passing cruiser found him ill and sailed him to the hospital in Rarotonga, where he passed away from cancer.

And the stories then became even more of an obsession for me, but I still refused to open the book. I had a dream, and I needed to make it come true.

•••

You see, the stories were told of other cruisers who would stop to visit Tom on his private hideaway. When they found him gone, they would still sign his guest book. If it looked like the hut he lived in was in disrepair, they would repair it.

As time went by, the guest book filled, but soon a passing cruiser dropped off another guest book, and it started to fill as well.

The legend of Tom Neale kept growing in my mind. Years later I read about cruisers who had stopped to visit and found half the hut blown down in a storm. They stayed for almost three months, and they rebuilt the hut. There were a couple of cans of beans that were starting to rust through, so they replaced the cans with new ones. And as people would come, they found it as he had left it years ago.

Eventually, the government of the Cook Islands decided the story was worthy of recognition, so they created a National Reserve for cruisers.

I read of the ceremony and wished I could have been there.

And then I decided it was time to stop dreaming and start living my dream. In 1991 I told Jody we were sailing to the South Pacific. Yes, we were going to stop in Tahiti. Yes, we were going to visit the Marquesas, and Samoa, and Tonga, but in my mind there was just one real destination.

Suverov.

Two days away from Suverov we were being beaten back by a storm. There was more rain than we'd seen before, even in the tropics. Then we saw the darkness on the horizon in front of us start to lighten. Soon we could actually see blue sky in front of us, even though rain and lightning were hitting all around us.

•••

As we sailed out from beneath the clouds we sailed into the warmth of a brilliant South Pacific day. The seas calmed, and just after dawn the next morning we entered the lagoon at Suverov Island. My first sight of the island was not disappointing.

It took us a day to dry out everything that had gotten soaked during the storm, but as the blankets and towels dried on the lifelines, I took out my book, grabbed a beanbag, and planted it firmly on the bow. As I read the book I lived Tom's adventure. I looked up and saw the beach he built his hut on. I saw where he'd fallen and hurt his back, struggling to get back into his boat.

And one day I got Jody and our two companions together, and we went ashore and helped rebuild the stone dock that had been torn apart in the last storm.

For days after I finished the book, I would sit and look out at the island, recalling passages. I traveled by dinghy across the lagoon, and I visited a small atoll where I found a large driftwood log described so perfectly by my friend Tom (as I often thought of him), sitting right where it was all those years ago.

I didn't share my feelings much with the rest of the crew. I couldn't. How do you share a dream?

And it was then I realized just how much cruising meant to me as a way of life. Most people dream their whole lives about doing something like that, and I had made my dream come true.

I still have a few books left that I plan on reading, where they were written! Go and live your dream!

Pearls before swine

><----

*I*had heard the phrase for years, but it wasn't until recently that I realized, 'twas I of which they spoke.

It all started about 10 years ago. Jody and I were sailing out of Apia, Western Samoa, on our way to Pago Pago in American Samoa, to provision for a voyage up to Hawaii. It was the end of the season in the South Pacific, and we planned on spending a couple of months in the Line Islands on the way.

As we made our way around the island, the seas kept building. The further we went around, the higher the seas and winds, and it was right on the nose, of course.

The island we were rounding was Upolu, Western Samoa. We checked the charts and found a bay called Fagaloa that we could run into and get out of the weather until morning. We figured we could get an early start the next morning and maybe get a little break.

As we made our way around the bend and into the bay, we found ourselves entering a scene from South Pacific. This place had to be Bali-Hai. It was absolutely one of the most beautiful bays we had ever seen. The bay was a deep, deep blue ringed by bright turquoise where the water was shallow. That was ringed by a brilliant white beach which, itself, was edged with a stand of tall and regal looking palm trees, which was, in turn, backed by a dark green jungle. About a quarter of a mile behind the green was a rugged cliff that climbed up into the clouds, and a waterfall that fell the complete distance, which looked to be hundreds of feet, into a blue stream that lead to the bay. It was perfect.

Just off the shore was a small group of dugouts with some of the locals who were fishing. As the LOST SOUL anchor dropped in the 40 feet of crystal blue water, one of the dugouts made its way over to us. We smiled and waved them aboard.

The first to board the boat was a Polynesian god. I swear I heard Jody gasp as he came up the steps. He was built like you imagine Adonis would have been built, and walked with a natural grace that said royalty. His jet black hair was long and worn down his back in a ponytail, and his upper body was completely covered with a tattoo.

In the old Polynesian culture, a tattooed upper torso indicated the first son of the Matai, or chief, of a village.

He told us that we were not permitted to anchor in the bay; that it was off-limits to non-natives. His English was very good. We told him how the weather around the corner was very unsettled and asked if there was any way we might be allowed to spend one night in his bay. We offered to pay for the anchorage and he was obviously insulted. I quickly changed the offer to making a donation to the village's church. He seemed to like this option, but obviously disliked taking anything from off-islanders. He agreed to a donation to the church in exchange for some food which the villagers would bring out to the boat. They asked for $80, we offered $20, and we settled on $40.

About an hour later, a dugout paddled out in the dusk and handed us a plate covered with a cloth. We thanked the men who brought it out, and Jody brought it below as they paddled towards shore. Once below, she took the cover off the dish.

It was a fishhead.

A fishhead? What the heck were we supposed to do with a fishhead? Was this some kind of insult? We give them good money and they give us a fishhead?

We dumped the fishhead out the porthole in the galley, and the rest of the night we derided the people of the village for their joke.

In the morning, we hoisted anchor and headed out. It was a beautiful place, but we'd been insulted and were glad to be leaving.

A couple of years later, we were sailing into Taaha in French Polynesia with my friend Curt. We'd caught a 180-pound marlin and called a man who ran a small resort on an outlying motu. He said if we brought the fish in, he'd get a local to clean it and trade us a good meal for the fish. Once we anchored, we loaded the marlin in the dinghy and took it ashore. As we stood around watching the local Polynesian clean the fish, we offered him his choice of cuts for his labors. He smiled and thanked us, and asked Charles, our host, if it would be all right to take the head.

Jody and I stood there kind of astounded. Why would he take the fishhead when he could have any part he wanted?

"That's the most prized portion of a fish in Polynesia," was his reply.

In other words, it was a pearl that had once been cast before us.

A voyage is like life

*C*an you imagine if everyone's life was judged on where or how it ends? You know what I mean. If everything a person has done in his or her lifetime meant nothing more than where it lead to when the time has run out, it would all be kind of silly, wouldn't it?

Well, a voyage is pretty much like life itself. It's not where the voyage is heading that is important. No, rather, it is what happens along the way; during that lifetime, during that voyage. You know, there are people out there who are in a hurry for it to be over. They are in a hurry to reach their destination. Pretty sad, isn't it?

Unfortunately, every voyage does end. If there is a sad part to cruising, that would be it. Every voyage, like every life, will come to an end. And at the end of the voyage, there is always a touch of sadness. It has passed. The adventure that you dreamed and created is behind you, never to be re-lived.

Oh, you can retrace your steps. You can even plan the same stops, the same time of departure, and even the same crew, but it will never be the same. You have been there, done that. Each time you depart, you will find new adventure.

In the past 30 years, I have sailed to Catalina Island literally hundreds of times. Yet, I can't think of any two trips that were the same. Oh, I've had the same weather.

I've done it over the same number of days, even on the same dates (different years, of course), but each trip, each voyage brought its own adventure. I still get the same feeling of excitement as I pull out of the slip that I felt the first time I went over, so many years ago. I still feel the same small thrill when I see that my anchorage is empty and waiting for me. In the wintertime, when we are the only boat in an anchorage that holds 400 boats in the summer, I love to just sit on the deck, looking out at the beauty, and watch the seagulls vie for a closer perch to my boat, in case we might drop something overboard.

I think that is the beauty of the cruising lifestyle; that certain knowledge that you will experience a new life's adventure every time you leave port, and if you don't, you know you'll find tranquility in its stead.

After all these years, and after all the tens of thousands of miles I have been able to cruise, each time I untie the docklines I still get that same feeling of excitement, that same glow inside that lets me know that I am alive and about to embark on another adventure.

It may just be a four-hour sail to Catalina, or a two-week crossing to Hawaii, or a voyage down the coast and through the Panama Canal, or around the world. It doesn't matter. The voyage is the thing. The knowledge deep inside that, in the time between untying the docklines and re-securing the boat back in her slip, there will be an adventure.

Recently, this has been brought into focus by two sailors who lived through some true ordeals, after leaving for "a three-hour sail." Unlike Gilligan, these men both underwent life-changing times aboard their boat. One Vietnamese man set sail for Catalina from Long Beach, California.

Literally, a four-hour sail. Three months later he was rescued off the coast of Costa Rica. When the Navy took him off the boat, he had enough food aboard to live comfortably. He was dismasted and had drifted south for all that time, and he was quite healthy and happy living off the sea. He captured sea birds by baiting them with pieces of the fish he'd catch. He cooked using wood he tore from the interior of his vessel. All he wanted when they picked him up was some help fixing his mast, so he could go on. He was still enjoying the voyage!

Another gentleman sailed his 22-foot sailboat out of Key West and was also dismasted. He got caught in the Gulf current and was found, half dead, four months later off South Carolina. He had not fared quite as well as the other man.

The point? Simple. No matter how small a voyage you are contemplating, it could turn into an epic, life-altering adventure.

The better prepared you are for these adventures, the better you will fare. Had these men had the basic tools of seamanship, like a radio, flares, or an EPIRB, what happened would never have transpired. But no matter how you look at it, they did have a true life-altering adventure.

So the next time you are going out for a little daysail, don't be in a hurry to get to the end. The voyage is like life itself. It's not what you find at the end, it's the voyage. Enjoy the ride!

Quiet time

———————➤◄———————

*I*t's quiet right now. For the last few hours I have been
sitting in the main saloon of the LOST SOUL and going
over pilot charts, navigation charts and cruising guides.
The planning may be the best part of a voyage.

In the planning stage everything is perfect. There are
no storms, no rude harbormasters with their hands out.
There is just me, my charts and my dreams.

I pulled out the pilot chart for the South Pacific to reaffirm
the departure date I had set in my mind. Yes . . . it would
work. If we left Hawaii in early May we should enter the
Line Islands in May, and that would give us a good month
or so visiting Palmyra, Fanning and Christmas before heading south to Pago Pago to supply.

To supply in Pago Pago . . . it still gives me a chill,
even though I have been there a few times. Something out
of Adventures in Paradise. Only now, 40 years after dreaming about it while watching it on a small black and white
round screen TV, it's a reality.

I pull out my old charts of the area. Let's see; where do
we want to anchor? Over here they have that big emergency
buoy. Remember when you drifted back into that during
the storm of 1992? Or was it in '93, on our way back from
Niuatoputapu? Yeah, that was it.

Hey, and here are the times marked for our crossing
down to the Vava'u Group in Tonga. Remember the night,

with Jody and what was her name . . . oh yeah, Ali. What a great night. The stars were as bright as I've ever seen them. Anchored in Niafu that night, I remember thinking that, if I were to die right then I would have been happy. What a life.

And then I saw a small tattered chart sticking out from under the Samoa/Tonga charts. Where's this? Oh, I remember. We found this chart in a small shop on the island of Tinos, in Greece. It's so beat up and weathered. It showed us that there was a good anchorage on the south side on Thira. I can remember how the rain was falling as we pulled in. That's why the chart's so tattered.

That was a great anchorage. Calm, clear nights, and days spent wandering the ancient streets of Santorini.

Sitting back I can smell the slight diesel/kerosene smell that has been a part every boat I have ever sailed. Closing my eyes, I can imagine I am sitting at anchor in Ibiza, or outside the Hawaii Yacht Club, or stern-tied to Papeete. Each place was paradise. Each was better than the last.

But now I have a new adventure to plan. New places to explore, and hopefully to have the same feelings I had in Antigua, Pago Pago, Greece. There is excitement in the planning, as there is in the accomplishing.

And so I break out a new chart. This one is unmarked. It has no times and dates showing when we crossed here. That's because it's somewhere we have never been.

And isn't that the real beauty of cruising? That, no matter where you have been, there are always new places to go to.

So now I have to get down to the nitty-gritty. It starts

with a one-day sail. It always starts with a one-day sail. And each daysail ends, and a new one begins. Before you know it, you are sailing on the opposite side of the earth from where you started. But each day is a new day. Each day brings a new adventure. The day we leave our homeport will be exciting. The first new day of our voyage.

Waking at an anchorage, or waking out at sea, whichever it is, I know the feeling that will be deep inside of my chest. A mixture of excitement, anxiety and pure joy. The excitement of discovery, the anxiety of not knowing what will befall us between this dawn and sunset, and the joy of knowing we have charted our voyage to take us to places that will change our lives.

So, hopefully, someday I will sit again like this; in the saloon of the LOST SOUL, smelling the smells and feeling the feelings of past voyages. Only the next time, I will be thinking back on what occurred on this voyage, while I plan the next.

Bon Voyage!

The perfect moment

I was dreaming I was anchored in Suverov Island in the Northern Cooks. It's my favorite dream. A crystal clear lagoon, the sun is shining, and the brilliant white sand of the motu is just a few hundred feet away. Just as I was about to dive in for a swim I heard Jody calling from a distance.

"Bob, you're on."

On? On what? Then, slowly, the dream started to fade, and the reality of a gale blowing us from the Azores to Gibraltar came back.

Reality! What a concept!

It was four in the morning. Time for my watch. We'd been fighting cold and bad weather since leaving the islands, almost three days earlier. When I was last on watch, the winds were blowing over 40 knots.

I pushed myself away from the bulkhead I was jammed against, and managed to pull on my sweats. The boat was heeled well to starboard, and just standing was an ordeal. I didn't want to get up. I wanted this all to go away, like a bad dream or something.

I made my way out of the aft cabin and into the main saloon. Two new bruises were added to my body as I made my way through the dark interior of the LOST SOUL.

In the galley the flame was on under the coffee pot. It was just like Jody to think of having the coffee ready for me.

Wedging my overly large butt against a bulkhead, I grabbed my favorite cup (I found it in a small shop in Tonga years earlier) and filled it with the rich, dark brew.

It took a bit of juggling to get the full cup up the companionway steps, but I managed to do it. As I emerged from the cabin I saw Jody strapped in behind the wheel. She was wearing her foulies and was jammed between the mast and the wheel, with her feet on the wheel to steady herself.

She was smiling.

Here we were, on the third day of a storm in the North Atlantic. It was two in the morning, cold and wet, and she was smiling.

"What a great night!" she exclaimed. "Look, Orion is so clear you can even see the smaller stars!"

I sipped my coffee and looked around. Stars? Who wants to look at stars? We're hundreds of miles from land and it's blowing stink. The seas are knocking us around like we are Mike Tyson's date, and the decks are slimy with cold saltwater.

I looked over at Jody and she had this big grin on her face.

"The wheel's all yours" she said, as she stood and unhooked her tether. "The winds have been abating a little, they are down to 30 knots and coming around. I let the sails out a little bit."

And with that she headed down below.

I put on my harness and hooked my tether to the base of the mast.

As I wedged myself in I looked out to sea. It was beautiful. The moon was glinting off the water, and the seas were actually starting to calm a little. I looked at the sails, and they were still reefed, but now they were on the first reef point, instead of the second, as I'd left it hours ago.

In the next hour the winds dropped from 30 knots to around 20. Instead of blowing tight out of 40 degrees, now they were almost 90 degrees. I let out the final reef, and fully unfurled the headsail. Life was good!

For the next hour I was probably one of the happiest people on earth. The winds moved around to come from behind us, and were blowing steady at 18 knots. After days of beating into a blustery cold storm, all of a sudden we were on a downwind run.

The sunrise watch has always been my favorite, but this particular morning it was spectacular. I went below and started the coffee and woke Jody. A few minutes later she emerged from below with a hot cup in her hand.

Neither of us said anything. We just sat there, watching nature do things that only she can do. The brilliant sky reflected off the water, and the LOST SOUL was cutting through it like a thoroughbred racer.

This was our reality. It was our life, and our dream. How many times can a person live a perfect moment? Existing in a moment when all things come together to make the feel, sight, smell and taste of life so real?

Fight a storm, sail an ocean, live through adversity, and feel the overwhelming relief when the battle is over. Then enjoy the fruits of your labors. Where else in life can you accomplish these feats?

For the next hour Jody and I sat in silence as we lived

one perfect moment after another. End to end, over and over. No words. Just perfection. Nothing could improve it.

Then the bilge alarm went off. We were back into reality. I went and unstuck the bilge switch, Jody took the wheel, and we waited for the next "perfect moment."

The dream is still there

O kay, so it was a pretty near perfect crossing. We'd
left Fatu Hiva and the Marquesas behind us, and
for the last four days we had been sailing in paradise. There
were 18-20 knots of wind coming from over our shoulder,
the main, mizzen, staysail and headsail were out, and we
were making a good eight knots in calm seas. It couldn't get
much better.

Just after dawn on the fifth day we spotted Manihi in the
Tuamotus. Andy won the beer for sighting land first, but I
think he cheated, because he climbed the mast to do it. That's
taking unfair advantage of an ageing and size-impaired captain, whose last trip up the mast was about 20 years and 50
pounds ago.

But it didn't matter. I had been dreaming of visiting the
Tuamotus since I started sailing. If there is one place that
sets a sailor's mind in first gear, it has to be seeing pictures
of those one thousand coral reef atolls just laying in the
crystal blue waters of the South Pacific.

In the 4,000 miles we'd sailed to this point in our South
Pacific expedition we had learned a lot. I learned that, even
though you may have been sailing for years, it just isn't like
what you'd been preparing for.

All of the magazines I'd read told me that we would hit
mountainous waves, hellacious storms and fight the prover-
bial dragon to cross the seas. Being a typical dunderhead,

I believed what I'd read, and was prepared for a truly monumental voyage. Now, here we were about to enter my dream island, and all that transpired to that point seemed abysmally easy.

As we turned to enter the lagoon I put Andy up the mast to watch our entrance (that'll teach him to take my beer!) and we slowly passed into the deep blue lagoon of our first tropical atoll. It was paradise.

I checked the charts for a good anchorage, and found a small motu with a white sand beach, and lots of coconut palms. After we watched the anchor set in the crystal clear water it was time for a swim. We could hardly wait to swim up onto the pure white sand beach.

Now, if this were a novel, it would be at this point where the poo-poo would hit the old mix-master. I honestly expected it. You know, maybe a hotel on the other side of the reef would boot us out, or a pissed-off landowner would tell us to skedaddle. After years of dreaming about this very second, I figured it couldn't actually be happening.

But folks, guess what? It still exists. Paradise is more than a mere state of mind. It is sitting out there just waiting for you to get there.

The reality of it is, the nightmare is getting ready to go. Cutting the lines and casting off is the beginning of a dream.

In the over 25 years that I have been cruising I have found one very basic truth. You've seen it on the T-shirts, but it still holds true. Your attitude is the difference between adventure and an ordeal. That and a little planning.

Sure it's crowded in Papeete, what do you expect? Over 1000 cruisers a year pass through there. But because of that you know you can find just about anything you need for you or your boat there, right? So if you don't like crowds, just go to Tahaa which isn't crowded yet, or Mopelia or Maupiti.

Looking for even smaller crowds, like maybe some truly desolated islands where you can be by yourself? Well, there are places like the Phoenix Islands, and even the Marshall and Solomon Islands are rarely visited.

Okay, when you sail Greece in prime cruising season it's crowded, but only in the more popular resort islands. Do some exploring and you'll find uncrowded islands even in paradise. If it's crowded, just leave. It's easy. Your house floats, remember?

Adjust the sail

I was staring at the headsail for five or six minutes before I realized I was daydreaming. I do that a lot once I get into cruising mode.

With me, cruising mode takes approximately three days before it sets in. It's a state of mind in which, for no apparent reason, your thoughts drift off into flights of pure fancy and fantasy. You know you have achieved it when you can hear, somewhere in the dim recesses of your mind, that you are being called for your watch, and you can't remember if the growling in your stomach is for breakfast or dinner.

It's as if you are in limbo. Non-cruisers always ask, "What do you do when you're at sea for weeks at a time?"

I can recall day after day of living the most exciting adventures, while kicking back on a downwind run to the Tuamotus or the Azores. Reality and fantasy blend into whatever book you are reading, and time dissolves.

After you have been at sea a few days the only importance there is to time is if you want to take a noon sight. Depending on how your watches fell, morning can be anywhere from dawn till noon. Underway you find being able to sleep is an asset. It makes the crossings go faster.

Once awake, you grab a book, nestle yourself into a comfortable nook, and delve into worlds far from the vessel you are on. While underway it is not strange to read three or four books in a week. The beauty of the lifestyle is, as you read each book you get drawn into it as if you live the adventure you are reading.

When the weather starts to kick up, your real life adventure takes over from the imagined. You find that weather that would have kept you in port back home, now turns on the excitement. Many say that the adventure truly begins when something goes wrong. As the signs of turbulent weather begin, you sense things that you never would have noticed before. A slight shift in the wind, and you are alerted to a change. You are a part of the immediate surroundings.

And when you get through it! Ha, then you know that you are really alive. When the winds are blowing on your bow, and the sea is soaking everything on board, you may curse the gods that turned the weather against you (and probably will!). But these gods are smarter than we mere mortals. A lot smarter. They know that the feeling of accomplishment achieved by overcoming adversity is the most fulfilling feeling a human can have. And they know the harder the adversity, the more intense the feeling of achievement.

Like when you read a great novel, the hero must dive into the depths of hell in order to achieve greatness. A story with no strife, or a life without struggle, cannot create a feeling of greatness. Sailing through turbulent seas can be this way.

A voyage goes from day to day, month to month, and year to year, building on what has happened. Most voyages start by heading somewhere safe. A cruising ground of some familiarity, where a new captain feels in control. You will notice that, as the months of a cruise extend to years, the destinations get a little more exotic. Most cruisers that we have met underway sail to places they never thought they would be going when they first set out. Once they have proven to themselves that they can depend on their personal strengths, they start sailing off the beaten path.

Looking back to a first cruise will usually put a smile on any cruiser's face. To think about that first leg, with all of the anxieties that went into the preparation, is so trivial in retrospect.

A new cruiser will look for a harbor that has plenty of other boats in it, so he can anchor where it's safe. Experienced cruisers will seek out the less used, remote anchorage, and anchor safely.

Whenever I am asked, "What it is really like once you cut the lines and get out there?" I find it a very easy thing to convey, so that anyone can understand what it means to cruise as a way of life. When I am working at trying to get back to the sea and the cruising life, it seems to me that the life of a cruiser isn't real. It seems as if it is just a dream. Now I have to make the biggest decision of the day. The headsail seems to be luffing a little up near the leading edge, and if I snugged it a little it might give us a bit more speed.

Yeah, I think it would. "Hey, Jody, remind me to snug up the jib a little later, will you?"

No matter where you go . . .

I half felt someone shake me, and for a minute I forgot where I was. As I opened my eyes, I heard Patrick whisper, "Hey man, 10 minutes and you're on."

It was 5:50 in the morning and the sun was about to come up. I walked through the creaking main saloon in the twilight of dawn with the kerosene lights casting a warm glow through the room, and felt the boat heel to port with a little gust of wind. The smell of coffee blended with the aroma of the kerosene, an alcohol stove, and the mildew of a thousand days at sea. As I poured the coffee into my favorite mug, I looked through the porthole and was transfixed. The horizon was a brilliant orange and gold. We were 150 miles off the coast of Guatemala, and that day was the most unreal sunup I can ever recall.

Today, over 20 years later, I can still recall that feeling. The way it felt to walk on deck of the 74-foot square-rigged tops'l schooner STONE WITCH and take the large tiller. The breeze over my shoulder, the telltales whipping, letting me know when to adjust the sails. The feeling of accomplishment, and even more so, pride, as we moved 50 tons of canvas, wood, and steel through the water with just the wind and our sweat.

It's true that you do not change when you go to sea. You are still the same person you always were. The only difference is, for many, it brings out a part of you that you never knew. I have never known anyone whose life was not improved by going to sea.

For some reason unbeknownst to me, many people treat the planning of going cruising as if they were planning to die.

Just check it out. They sell their homes, say goodbye to their friends, cancel their magazine subscriptions (aagh! that hurts!) and do everything but buy a plot.

Why? They're just going cruising, right? Your life doesn't end when you cut the lines and say adios to friends and neighbors. Wherever you are heading, you can call home. That's why cruising is such a great way of life. You get to go out and experience what it's like to live in all types of environments. In Polynesia, you learn to find the ripe fruits for your lunch on trees. In Greece, you can live as people have lived for many millennia. In Antarctica, you can live like a penguin if you want. But no matter where you go, you are still there, with yourself.

Have you ever met anyone out cruising who is a real grump? You know, the kind of person who walks into a room looking like he smells something bad? Well, you can bet your backup bilge pump he was the same back home. You can't run away from yourself. If anything cruising introduces you to yourself. There's nothing like a few hundred days jammed together in a vessel the size of a large storage shed, with nothing but water surrounding you, to get to know the real you.

We have all heard the tales of couples who have been married for 25 years or so taking off to cruise the world, only to end up in divorce court six months later. After living together all those years, they can't figure out what happened. For 25 years they saw each other four hours a day and on the occasional weekend. All of a sudden, they are forced to spend 24 hours a day together, sometimes in stressful situations. You get to know your crewmates very well, very fast.

Fortunately, the majority of people who opt for the cruising way of life do so because they are pretty mellow to begin with. In most cases, people who drop the dock lines and sail off into the sunset find that they actually like each other better once they are away from the battle of trying to exist, and start to really live.

Life is just like a cruise. It doesn't matter how or where it ends, it's the journey to reach the end that counts. You have to take every day for what it is. And you will notice that each day you awaken, as you cruise through the world, and through your life, you always wake up with the same person. Yourself. You don't change once you leave. The little things that annoyed you when you were at home will still annoy you. The thrills you get are the same underway, only better.

The big difference is the joy you get from the small things you never had time to notice. For every cruiser, it's something else.

For me, it will always be that feeling I first encountered at 5:50 a.m., March 27, 1978, aboard the STONE WITCH.

The little moments
➤◄

We had been anchored in the lagoon at Fanning Island for a couple of days when we realized we were running short on gasoline for our outboard. The closest fuel was 120 miles away at Christmas Island. We'd noticed a Land Rover parked under a tarp on our hike through the little village, which had seemed a little odd, since there were not only no roads, but not enough land on the motus to make one. When we asked if they had any fuel they proudly pointed to a full 55-gallon drum. It seems that the Australian government had given them the Land Rover and fuel as a gift, but they had no place to use it.

In a few minutes, they agreed to trade some canned goods and food for five gallons of gas. I hurried back to the boat and started to gather some goodies. I knew they hadn't seen a supply ship in over a year because we had been asked to bring some bags of rice and flour with us from Christmas Island when we sailed in, so anything would have been welcome. I wanted to give them the better end of the deal, so I dug deep into our supplies. I came up with some canned peaches, pears and fruit cocktail. Then I added some corn flour, canned butter, and salt. A couple cans of Spam were added to the mix (to them it was like a side of roast beef) and also an extra few pounds of sugar. We gathered some balloons and an extra Frisbee we had for the kids and some hair ribbons for the women. It was a good package.

But I wanted to do a little something extra to let them know how much I appreciated the fuel, so I dug deep into the bottom of the refrigerator and brought out a five-pound brick of cheddar cheese. We loaded everything into the dinghy and headed back to the village.

Our arrival was like a party. The entire population of the village, all ten of them (OK, so it was a pretty small place) were there to help with the dinghy. We walked over to a tree stump and started to lay out the goodies. Their eyes lit up when we pulled out the canned fruit. They got even more excited when they saw the sugar and butter, and when the kids saw the balloons they squealed with delight. Meanwhile, the women were busy dividing the hair ribbons.

Then it was time for the piece de résistance. The cheese. I pulled out the brick and handed it to the matai of the village. He looked at it for a second as if it were from another planet, smiled politely, and walked us to the gas can. I was actually a little disappointed that he hadn't gotten a little more excited.

We siphoned the gas and headed back to the boat, as the kids played on the beach with the balloons. The rest of the day was spent wasting our newfound gas.

That evening, just at sunset, Father Bermond, the priest for the Line Islands, came to call. We'd given him a ride over from Christmas Island and he was staying on board. He was grinning real wide and shaking his head.

"What's up?" I asked, "What's so funny?"

"Well, you know that cheese you gave the head of the village?" he asked.

"Yeah, it was cheddar. I thought they'd love it but they just looked at me real weird when I gave it to him. Do you have any idea why?"

"As a matter of fact, I do," he waited a second, and then went on. "Have you seen any cows on any of these islands?"

I just shook my head slowly. "No. I can't say that I have. Why?"

"Well, the old boy waited until you left to check out what you gave him, because he had no idea what it was. Once you were back at the boat, he and some of the other villagers tried to open the plastic wrapping. When they finally cut it the pure rich aroma of a fine cheddar cheese wafted up to them," he smiled again, and then went on. "They thought it was something that had gone bad. They took it out back and fed it to the hog."

Of course, Father Bermond was more than merely bemused. It seems that, being French, he just loved cheese, but hadn't had any in a very long time.

That night, over a pig bowl of macaroni and cheese, we had a big laugh over it all. But there is a point to this story. In order to understand people, you need a common ground.

Sometimes we just take for granted all that we see, and have seen, as we cruise the world. In order to more fully enjoy it, we have to take the time to "get inside the head" of the people we visit.

What more joy could there be than introducing a remote islander to ice cream, or the magic of seeing himself on video tape? It's the little moments like this that make cruising the best way of life on earth.

A cruisers' beach party

————▶◀————

*I*t was an impromptu beach party in Antigua. Eighteen cruisers from around the world had gathered to greet the New Year at a beach bistro. There was a prince from Malaysia (he picked up the tab, thank God), a much-pierced, skinhead musician from England, an old biker from the US, a young couple from New Zealand, a café owner from Scotland, a business woman from Germany, two sisters from Australia, a scientist and a couple from South Africa. Some were single, some were married, and some were gay. We were cruisers, so we were family.

All of us were doing something that only a small percentage of people on earth will ever do. We sailed the world under wind power, an adventure that equalizes all who attempt it.

There are very few true adventures left on this earth. Only out here, in Neptune's kingdom, do we all become equal. There is something about fighting a 100-foot wall of water, and coming out on top (literally) that brings us into one group.

There have been plenty of doodads made available to make a cruiser's life easier, but in the end it still comes down to just one thing: surviving in the most inhospitable environment on earth—the sea.

We all have this picture in our mind of pristine beaches with tall palm trees and crystal blue lagoons, or pulling into ancient Greek ports. This is what drives us to cruise. But the truth is, before we sit on that pristine beach, or visit the ancient worlds, we must fight our way across thousands of miles of a very unforgiving ocean. This is the adventure. If it was easy, everyone would be doing it, right?

Knowing that you, with just the wind and your self-reliance, sailed there, makes your visit all the more sweet. You are not a tourist.

The cruisers you meet along the way? They're your family. You find that the things which used to be important, like status, what kind of car you drive, and what you do for a living, pale when compared to the realities of how a person handles himself in a real crisis. If you meet someone who has cruised a while, there is automatic mutual respect. You know what it took for you to get there, and you know the people you meet have passed that test.

The sea is the big equalizer, and all who sail her waters belong to a select group. Membership is free, but anything but easy, and once attained you belong for life. Good sailing!

PART 5

The best of *Latitude & Attitudes* editorials

As you may well have discerned from these writings, upon my return from an extended voyage, I created a magazine for people like myself, who live and dream of the long voyage. Most of the essays you have read were originally published in *Latitudes & Attitudes* over the years.

The following essays were written as editorials, and we have decided to include them in this collection.

No explanation

We gotta be nuts, you know? Check it out . . . just what is it we all have in common? I mean besides smelly feet? Well? You know what it is? A desire to sell all of the stuff we have worked our whole life to gather about us, and then to move into an area slightly larger than a jail cell.

Not only that but, once we have managed to convince our significant other it will be fun, we cast off our lines and sail this vessel out into the most inhospitable environment on earth. The ocean.

Hey, it's true! Where do you find things that eat men (and women) whole? Only in the ocean. Besides that, could you imagine if the sand dunes in a desert could form piles 100 feet high, and then fall on you? Well, that's pretty much what happens in the ocean, right?

But that isn't even the half of it. To make it a little more fun, how about we jam a couple of sticks in the vessel, and tie on a bedsheet or two. What kind of idiot can actually believe he can make twenty or so tons of plastic and steel go across an ocean with just wind power?

Okay, let's make it a little sillier. Let's put some electricity in these things. Sure, that's it! Electricity and salt water . . . what a great idea. That'll burn up the thru hulls a little faster . . . kewl!

We could add some weight to the bottom of these things,

so they'd drop to the bottom faster when filled with water, and maybe put some storage containers of sulfuric acid inside, in case we are able to roll it over. We could call these batteries!

That, in a nutshell, is what people who have no idea why we go cruising think. Really! It's true! They think we've slipped a cog or two. You know, a few fries short of a happy meal?

Of course there is the other side of the coin. Our side. Here's a sleek and ready sailboat, tied to the docks, filled with all the things that actually mean something to us. The feeling that fills you as you cast off to begin an adventure can only be understood by those who do it.

To face an adversary like mother nature, with the full confidence that you have been thorough enough in your preparations to be prepared for all instances. What better feeling could there possibly be?

Okay, there is one. The feeling when, after making your first crossing, you are pulling into your first distant anchorage. A fellow boater waves welcome, and you stand at the wheel, waving back. To those who have never completed such a voyage, it is pretty hard to explain what such a feat means.

Sure there are tests we will endure during our voyage. That's where the true adventure is. As I often say to Jody, the adventure begins when something goes wrong!

Oh, don't get me wrong. I love an easy sail. It's what we all look forward to. Days of drifting under a warm breeze, with the boat slicing through the water, on your way to a tropical paradise. What could be better, right?

Well, about the only thing better is the same scenario,

but after making your way through a storm and looking behind you to see the dark storm clouds and lightning, filled with self-assurance.

To feel like your blood is pumping, as if you have actually done something worthwhile, you have to fight the good fight! You need a worthy adversary! Not some wimp purser to snivel to!

Like I said, there are those out there who just can't understand why a person would ever leave a warm and cozy home, load all their stuff into a little boat, and sail off to face the same storms that Captain Cook and Tristan Jones faced.

To those who don't understand, there is no explanation. To those who do, none is needed.

Okay, 'nuff said. Let's go where the water's deep.

Cruising, what a concept

➤◄

*C*ruising, what a concept . . . to put all of your worldly belongings on a sailboat, haul up some canvas, and sail off into the sunset. Everybody dreams of doing it, but only a very few are ever really crazy enough to cast off the lines. This publication is dedicated to those of us who are just crazy enough to live this lifestyle, those of us who cram our lives into an area just a tad larger than the average jail cell, point a vessel toward the open sea, and truly believe that, with just the wind at our backs, we will actually see landfall on the other side of the horizon . . . those of us who have found the reality in our dreams.

Some 20 years ago, I sailed out of San Francisco aboard a topsail square-rigged schooner called STONE WITCH. Built and captained by my mentor, Alan Olsen, she had no motor, sported four 22-foot oars as her auxiliary power, and ran under kerosene running lights. We hauled the anchor by hand and raised the sails without winches. We drank tepid Kool Aid, lived off canned corned beef, and loved every damned minute of it.

And I fell in love with cruising.

Now I don't want you to get the wrong idea. I am not a purist. I enjoyed my initiation to cruising, but I learned from it. Times change and people do too. Now my favorite saying is, "I cannot recommend decadence as a way of life, but it works for me." People who substitute storage (or even bathtubs!) for engines are a few bricks short of a full load in my book. As I said, my first cruising was done the hard way, but in the intervening 20 years I have gone full tilt in the other direction. Such luxuries as a TV, VCR, SSB, radar, autopilot, and microwave are just the beginning. The man who invented the watermaker is a deity in my book, as is the man who came up with GPS. Solar panels fill my batteries so my icemaker won't let me down—there is nothing like the sound of ice tinkling in a glass at sunset as you cross the equator. The days of tepid Kool Aid have passed— and good riddance.

For almost 20 years I have lived aboard sailing vessels and cruised well over 75,000 miles. In just the past five years I have had the pleasure of sailing some 45,000 miles to the most beautiful places in the world. During this time, I have shouted, "I hate boats," a thousand times, sailed with idiots and geniuses, seen poverty and riches, and have been fortunate enough to join the family of cruising sailors— that stupid breed of human that spends weeks at sea in heavy weather, with water dripping into every orifice, and actually has a smile on his face when entering a storm-swollen harbor. To those who have never done it, you just can't explain what it's all about, and to those who have lived it, no explanation is needed.

Latitudes & Attitudes is dedicated to this family of crazies, and to the way of life we live. The idea was born during a hundred nights at sea and nurtured in small gatherings on beaches around the world. Input from cruisers met in far-flung ports has become a reality, and *Latitudes & Attitudes* is that reality. Welcome aboard. This is your magazine.

It is not published by Daddy Warbucks Industries or Acme Conglomerate Publishers. There's just me and a couple of cruising friends. If you like it let me know, and if you don't, tell me why.

Got milk?

>——————◄►——————

*H*ave you ever given any thought to trying to figure out just who the boating industry thinks "we" are?

I mean, just who is it the people who build boats and supply parts have in mind when they think of their customers?

Since I came back from our world cruise and started this silly magazine I have been constantly getting comments that go something like this from people in the industry who I talk to.

"Yeah, I've been getting your magazine for years. It's the only one I take home with me to read. I love it," they'd say.

I, of course, would then ask the obvious question, "Well, why aren't you advertising with us?"

To which they would most always reply, "Oh, your readers aren't our audience, but I love the mag!"

And they'd walk off leaving me standing there, dumbfounded.

The other day I was talking with a gentleman who is trying to start an all-sailing television network. As he stood there blathering on about how they have Gary Jobson "on board" and various other "famous" sailors, it hit me. After ten years in the industry I realized who "their" customers are. And guess what? It ain't us!

Ever since the first private yacht sailed into Buzzards Bay, the aim of the yachting community has been the yacht owner. Not the boat guy. Not the guy standing on the dock

●●

in ripped Levis and an old T-shirt. No, the aim of the marketplace is this mysterious yachtie, the cream of the crop, who stands at the rail of the yacht club with wife Buffy. In one hand he grips a recent copy of International Yacht, or some such mega book from a mega-buck outfit showing the latest multi-million dollar creations, and a martini tightly gripped in his other manicured hand, looking out at his new 85-foot Hinkley sloop.

I know when I started sailing I felt that was the world of sailing as well. The guys on the dock that met up at the bar for a cold one after sanding their boat, well, we were just peeking into the world of wealth, glitz and glamour.

As I walk through a boat show today, I see a lot hasn't changed.

Oh, the industry still seems to think their target audience is the multi-trillionaire. To prove this they point with pride at the America's Cup races and marvel at the millions of viewers who watch this snail race at sea. Their chests swell with pride as they point at the cream of the sailing crop. Boats owned by people like Rockefeller, Diamond Jim Brady and Andrew Carnegie.

But as they walk the docks, it's not Carnegie or Mellon who is crowding to see the latest creations.

It is us! It is the people who fight long and hard to earn a buck, so they can dream about one day sailing off into the sunset on their own boat.

Did you ever notice how real people have a hard time saying "yacht?" I know I do. I don't own a yacht. I own a boat. People sail boats, society sails on yachts.

The reality is the most visible people in yachting are the cream of the crop. It is a thin layer of cream, but they are there. The cream owns America's Cup boats. The cream own houses on the bay with mega-docks in front of them.

But it's the boat owners like us who keep the boating business alive. When you are down at the docks working on your boat, or anchored out for a weekend, how many mega-yachts do you see? I know on my dock everyone works pretty hard for their boat parts.

The cream floats on top, just in case you haven't ever noticed. It is just the top. What is holding all of that cream up there is a whole lot of not so rich milk. That'd be us. The milk.

Don't they ever notice that boats with a realistic price tag sell 100-1 over the beautiful mega-buck boats? Does it go unnoticed that when something goes on sale it sells better?

Sailors are just a segment of society who found they are happiest when out there on the water. They aren't out there because their dad left them a million bucks (but it would help!). They are out there because they work hard to fulfill a dream. The dream is cruising. The dream is kicking back on the deck of your boat while anchored in some distant bay, thinking back on what it was like before you got into the boating life.

Yeah, we may not be the cream of society, but we are the lifeblood of the sailing and cruising community.

So the next time you're walking the dock, look around you. Wave to your neighbor and enjoy the moment.

Who needs cream? Got milk!

Slay the dragon

————————➤◄————————

*T*oday has been one of those bad days. You know. We all get them. No matter what you try to do, it's wrong. No matter what the news, it's bad. Just a plain bad day.

And to top it off I have to write some inspirational words for my column. I am thinking this just plain ain't gonna work. I can't seem to get a good thought. Kinda like Peter Pan when he couldn't fly.

So what I think I'll do is reach down into my memory and see what kind of a good day I can dredge up from when Jody and I were out there sailing. If it works, this'll be an inspirational dissertation with meaning. If not, well, I guess you won't be reading this.

So I'm gonna reach behind me, to my copy of *Letters from the LOST SOUL*, the story of our greatest voyage, and see what happens when I open the page . . .

We had left Pago Pago to sail north to Hawaii. Our first leg couldn't have been much worse, kinda like today. We'd sailed out of Pago and to a neighboring island where, naturally, we hit the anchorage just after dark. As I put anchoring in a strange harbor after dark on my fun list just under finding out Manson was at my daughter's sweet sixteen party, you can imagine the funk I was in. Top this off with the fact that, when we awoke, we found we were less than 20 feet from a reef that was just under the surface, and we didn't know it was there.

Then the winds came. As any cruiser knows, the winds are always either too much or too little, but they are always on the nose. Such was the case on the morning we departed.

For the next 10 days we sailed into winds that increased to 25-30, then to 35, and finally to 40 knots. The direction? Pretty much the wind came out of where we wanted to go, Christmas Island.

Day after day we were beat up, as we sailed as tight on the wind as we could get. The boat slammed into waves until we thought she'd shake apart, and we held our course.

We had about another 600 miles to go to Christmas Island, and our steering was leaking. Not only that, but we were running out of transmission fluid. Then my dinghy sprung an air leak and was hanging limp off the stern. We couldn't wash dishes or make water because the boat was heeled over so far from the wind that the sink overflowed from seawater and the watermaker wouldn't work at that angle.

When we finally spotted the island, we were about ten miles off. We had to tack a few times to get in, but the feeling we had inside when the island came into view is something that I can still recall vividly. The winds were still blowing at about 35, but since they had subsided from the 45 they were blowing before, it seemed like a summer breeze.

The current was still taking us away from the island, but since we knew we would be anchored before nightfall, it didn't seem so bad.

As we tacked and sailed, and then tacked again, I started to actually feel a joy welling up inside. Pretty much the same feeling when I first approached Nuku Hiva after our 2,700 mile voyage from Mexico, or the first time I sailed into Radio Bay in Hilo, Hawaii, some 20 years earlier, on my first major ocean crossing. I felt happy.

I didn't dwell on the feeling at the time. I just remembered how good it felt. How proud I was of my boat, of Jody, and Luke and Joel, who'd sailed with us all the way from Papeete. We'd had adversity thrown at us again and again, and for almost 900 miles we were beat up, had things break and were about as uncomfortable as a cruiser could be, but it was over. Not only that, but we were, once again, about to enter a new paradise. A new cruising ground to be discovered.

You know, if there weren't any mountains there wouldn't be any valleys. If adversity wasn't to rear its ugly head now and then, how could we ever feel that thrill of accomplishment?

Official millennium editorial

———▶———

*O*kay, here it is. I managed to do the magazine's cover without even mentioning the new millennium, but my staff (both of them) wouldn't let me get away without doing something here.

At first I sniveled a bit. You see, it gets my gall that all the magazines are going to be doing some big bomb blast about the new millennium, like they invented it or something.

Hell, I'm writing this in September. You're probably reading it in December. It makes it hard to comment on something that's not even here yet.

But anyway, after some reflection, I guess this is a pretty kewl deal. I remember sitting in the back of my mom's station wagon some fifty years ago, thinking for the first time about 2000. Back then, in the 50s, we had all kinds of ideas of what it would be like. You know, satellites going around the earth, pocket radios, space shuttles; all those things that we know they'll never really have, right?

So here I sit, writing my story on a laptop computer, sending it to my office over a satellite. I had to stop for a second and answer my pocket-phone. In a few minutes I will wander topside and make sure my autopilot is handling everything okay, and maybe I'll pull in a little of my self-furling headsail.

Yeah, like I was saying. We had all kinds of ideas about

farflung things that could never happen. Sailing has changed hardly at all since the last century. What could change about something as basic as sailing? I ask you, what?

Let's see, wooden boats with canvas sails and iron men. That's the sailing scene in 1900. Of course there is this new stuff they call fiberglass. It might work okay for building boats. And then there is Dacron and the other world of modern fabrics they are making. Can you imagine how beautiful a full rigged bark would have been if they had invented spinnakers back then? Just think about it. A few hundred thousand feet of billowing nylon in a rainbow of colors.

But wait. There are no more barks. Now they have found a way to make boats sail into the wind! Can you imagine what they would have thought seeing a modern sloop sail 25° off the wind?

And what about things like radar, autopilots and GPS? What used to be the mark of a sailing man, his sextant, has now almost become a museum piece. Only the few of us who still know how to make a reduction still carry them, and then, mostly for the nostalgia of the old days.

Sailing is one of the few endeavors that have actually been around since the start of the last millennium, and a few millennia before that, as well.

You know, even thinking about all that has happened in the past 100 years, if you go back 1,000 years, there is still a connecting thread.

We sailors are a lucky lot. As we drift along on a soft tradewind, listening to the sound of the water as it trickles by the hull, we can imagine what our ancestors must have been thinking, 1,000 years ago. We still have a common bond with them. There is no doubt but that they got just as excited as we do when they saw a pod of dolphins or whales. As you turn to pull in your trailing fishing line next time, think about how, over 1,000 years ago, your predecessors were doing exactly the same thing, and having just the same thought. "Oh boy, fresh fish!"

I started this silly column with the intention of taking it to where sailing has gone in the past hundred years, and then maybe speculating on where it might go in the next 100 or even 1,000 years.

But that's not what sailing is all about. Nor is it what the millennium should be all about. It's the past!

Our relationship with our ancestors is still strong and tight. Every time you feel the wind start to push you toward your destination; every time you drop that hunk of iron tied to the string on your bow, you are merely a shadow of a sailor who did the same thing, probably in the very same spot, 100 years ago. And 1,000 years ago.

And you know the thing we should really be celebrating on this very auspicious occasion? It is the fact that 1,000 years from now, some sailor, just like you, will be dropping his hook in the same spot, and thinking the very same thing.

Here's to us!

Sexist? Me?

➤◄

*H*a, once more into the breach. It has come to my
attention that there are those out there who think
Latitudes & Attitudes is sexist. Can you imagine?

Yeah, really! I was standing there at the boat show, trying to get more suckers to subscribe to the rag, and some
lady looks down at our cover and says, "Why do you have
to put a half-clad, beautiful girl on the cover?"

As usual, I placed my size 13 into my pie-hole, and
said what I thought.

"Why would I put an ugly fat lady on the cover?"

"That's sexist!" she harrumphed, and started to walk
away.

"Hey," I said, trying to smooth her feathers, "we have
only had three covers with ladies on them, and we've had
three with men on the covers."

But by then she had wandered off to harass some other
unsuspecting fool. I stood there totally bummed out.

Am I sexist? I don't know. I was raised in a time when
there was no such thing. There were just people. The magazine business was easier then. Put a pretty woman on the
cover, it sells. *Cosmopolitan* does it, and they're kewl.
Vogue does it, and they're hip. I do it, and I'm a pig.

Maybe that's why I like to get out of the civilized world
and cruise. Out there, if I appreciate an attractive lady, it's
a compliment. Here, it's sexual harassment. Tell a woman

she looks good, and you could end up in jail. That makes sense, huh?

For the first four years of *Latitudes & Attitudes* I have chosen the covers very carefully, using a criterion of "What looks really good?"

By now we have had three covers with attractive ladies, three with men (I can't say if they are attractive or not, as I am not gay) and one with a couple. The other 20 have had boating scenes. As I worked the booth the rest of the weekend, I paid close attention to what was being said on the other side of the table.

After a while I was actually sorry I had. Oh, everybody seemed to really like the magazine, but never once did I hear it referred to as what I designed it to be—a realistic look at the world of the cruising sailor.

Oh, I heard irreverent, funny, risqué and provocative, but not real.

What I think escapes people is the fact that the whole magazine is written by cruisers, not by a staff. What we run is what we get sent. We don't shoot the pictures, not even the covers. They are sent in by cruisers. What you see on these pages is what is out there. If it offends, don't go out there. Don't blame us for showing it to you! If you want to stick your collective heads in the dirt, don't read *Latitudes & Attitudes*. Read *Reader's Digest*. They'll tell you what life is like in the "real world."

Okay. Now back to sexist. I could be. I believe there is a difference between men and women, and I revel in the difference. I still open the door for a lady. I have a hard time if a woman picks up a check. If I see a woman on the side of the road, I feel I should help her. Guess that makes me sexist.

I also think the Boy Scouts are for boys, and the Girls Scouts for girls.

On a boat there are some differences, no matter how much we try to ignore them. Somehow, on the majority (that's the key word here) of cruising boats, the man is the mechanic and the woman the provisioner. If the mechanic needs help, the provisioner helps. When the provisioner goes to the store, the mechanic tags along to give a hand. I don't see this as sexist. I know of cruising boats with crews of two women or two men, and of these one is usually the mechanic, and one the provisioner. Sexist? No, I think I'd call it logical.

Okay, back to what started all this. Our covers. We are a sailing lifestyle magazine. The covers are not political. They are meant to be attractive, and to sell more magazines. If a photo comes in with a bitchin shot of a boat under sail, or at anchor, I run it. If a cover comes in with an attractive lady or couple, I will run it. If a photo comes in with an attractive man, I will go to a head shrinker. I have never seen an attractive man.

It's not that I'm homophobic. Hell, for all I know, I might be gay! I've just never met a man I like that much, or found attractive!

So stop with the sexist stuff. Let's get real. When cruising, there is a chance you will see an attractive lady in (or out of) a bathing suit. If that offends, may I suggest a subscription to *Igloo Quarterly*?

We are a sailing and cruising magazine. Our covers are not there to make a statement, they are there to sell magazines. If I have a choice of two covers, one with an ugly fat man and one with an attractive lady, any guesses which one you'll see?

It's not about sex, it's about sailing.

So I'm going sailing!

The sacrifices I make

W here in the book does it say that just because some idiot can pound on a typewriter (or computer, in this case), he has wisdom dripping from every orifice? Huh, come on! Where?

The other day I'm reading (expletive deleted) and all of a sudden it hits me why I started this rag in the first place. It was because, after returning from cruising for a few years, everything I read seemed to, uh, let's see, how should I say this? Lack credibility?

Okay. So I set down the magazine and grabbed one of my own creations. *Latitudes & Attitudes.*

You know what? It seemed almost as bad.

I mean, what's up with all the products that we flaunt before the eyes of those who are seeking wisdom from us. We have the Bosun's Bag, where advertisers try to poison your minds by paying us to put their products before you. Then we have The Chandlery, where we try to show you new stuff you can't afford and, in all likelihood, don't need.

And if that isn't enough, you turn farther back in the book and here I am, touting all the neat stuff I crammed on the LOST SOUL during the refit. Of course the fact that I get all that paraphernalia at huge discounts, or, if I'm really lucky, free, because of the rag, doesn't enter into the story. It should. I am actually feeling a little guilty. Okay, so it's very little, but guilty nonetheless.

What I should say in the article is something like this: "I installed a Whazoo 5600 Kathorple valve on the boat to decrease flatulence. I chose this unit because Fred, the guy that makes them, gave it to me to try and convince my readers that they are needed on every boat. If I had to go out and pay real money to buy one, I probably wouldn't have gotten it."

Now don't go looking back at the article, because you won't find any reference like that in there.

Why isn't it there? Because, since starting this rag, I have had to look at things a lot differently. First of all, there are people out there who need a Whazoo 5600 because of excessive flatulence, and they need to know what's available. (How's that for justification, huh?)

Therefore it is kinda my duty to test it. That doesn't make me an expert on fixing flatulence. After all, I have only used the Whazoo 5600. Perhaps if I'd tried the Binford 5700 Kathorple valve it would have worked as well, or maybe better.

But no, since Fred over at Whazoo got to me first, I gotta tout this version.

Of course there are always the "purist" publications you can go to. *Practical Sailor* will be glad to show you all the differences between the Whazoo 5600 and the Binford 5700. Every little nut, every twinge, every minute little detail. They will leave no Kathorple unturned, in order to test every nuance of these items.

Of course you must be a slide-rule carrying engineer, or chew pure Starbuck's espresso grounds to keep from nodding off in the middle of the dissertation.

So what's the answer? After all, there has to be an answer, doesn't there?

BOB BITCHIN

NOT! There is no answer. When you read about some new flatulence relief valve, the first thing that should go through your mind is: Just how important is flatulence to me and my loved ones? Do I really need a Kathorple valve, or will a simple jar of Beano get me through a voyage?

It's my job to try and show you guys everything that's out there that can make your life easier. To do this I must make sacrifices. I have to go sailing a lot. I have to endure getting lots of free stuff, and/or great deals on goodies for my boat.

The LOST SOUL waterline is rising faster than a yard bill during haul-out, as I give my all to test the latest hammock or deck chair. I force myself to see how well a particular autopilot works, by setting it. I test it like a cruiser would. I use it. Is the refer working? I dunno. Maybe I'd better see how cold the beer is.

See the sacrifices I make for you?

And do I get any sympathy for all I am going through for my readers? I do not! My neighbors come down the dock and razz me for having this overabundance of stuff on my boat. They jeer at my new Whazoo 5600, and mock my new flatulence-free life.

And does it hurt me to have my friends harass and demean me like that?

Nope! Not in the least. I shall continue to make these sacrifices for boaters everywhere, until you guys figure out the truth. That all you need to go sailing is a boat. The rest is window dressing.

You gotta do what you want

━━━━━━━━━━━━▶◀━━━━━━━━━━━━

*T*his editorial started out as an answer to the first
letter we have this month in our "From the World"
titled "It Ain't Easy Being Sleazy."

When we got the letter everyone in the office had a big
laugh. Yeah, right, like there really are people out there
who really think you must wear a harness and tether at all
times while at sea. People who feel you should always have
a life vest on, or always wear spiffy deck shoes, and fear for
your life while cruising. We figured this letter must be a put
on. All of us have lived aboard and cruised, and it seemed
ludicrous that there might be someone out there who actually got upset because someone would sail without a harness or deck shoes.

That night, as I gave it a little more thought, I realized
that this dude was serious. He really did think all that, and
more. Then I started asking myself why. What could cause
a person to think like that? Then I started asking myself
what can I do to help show the fallacies in such thinking? I
mean, I've made a couple of dozen major ocean crossings,
and I know that I'm not qualified to tell someone else what
to do, so what would make this guy think he was? And then
it hit me . . . he knew what was right for everyone because
someone told him the right way to do it, and they probably
did so in print.

It's obvious that some folks spend a little too much time

reading magazines like Anal Retentive Sailor and books like *The Perfect Storm*. Not only do they read them, but they actually believe that this is what they will find once they cut the docklines.

Hey, wake up! It's not like that out there! If it were nobody in their right mind would go. Sure the magazines tell you to wear the latest Sure Stick Green Water Sailing Shoes. Of course they tell you to always wear a tether and life vest. Who do you think paid for all those pretty pages of advertising?

This is not a sport, dude . . . this is a friggin' lifestyle! You are meant to enjoy it! It is not an episode of Survivor! The person who wears the most safety gear doesn't get an extra ration of water or an Oreo cookie! The first person to down a beer doesn't get sent home. This is real life, and it's here to be enjoyed.

Go barefoot at sea? You bet. One of the highlights of my life is when I cruised for a full year and never once put on a pair of shoes. Bare feet on wet teak are the original answer to non-skid! Go swimming mid ocean? I can't think of anything that feels better. I can't imagine crossing the equator and not jumping in on the imaginary dotted line. It is one of the many joys of cruising.

It is not our job to sit here and tell people what to do, any more than it's our job to go telling folks to go without safety gear. We aren't telling people to do anything. We are just telling them what it is really like out there, and it's written by people who are out there, doing it, not by editors who are in an office telling you what to think and how to act out there so you can be "in."

Yeah, there are safety issues. So what? We have to assume that every person who goes to sea has the common sense God gave 'em. On the LOST SOUL, we have a rule that no one stands night watch without a harness and tether. That's our level of comfort. If your level of comfort is to wear an all-weather, man-overboard body suit day and night, kewl . . . do it. Just don't preach to me that I'm not doing it right because I have a different comfort level with my safety.

Every skipper sets his own rules when cruising. If you're a racer, the committee can set the rules. But magazine editors do not set the rules. Nor do people who write books. Every person has to use his or her intellect to glean the facts from what they read, and to find their own safety comfort level.

And what is this fixation with "in your face partying?" Sounds like maybe someone has seen too many baseball ads on TV. To repeat myself, we don't preach anything to anyone, we simply print stories that are written by active cruisers who are out there. We do not assign stories to editorial staff that sit around an office. We print stories sent in from people who are out there, living the lifestyle. Anyone who has ever cruised knows the joy of meeting with other cruisers in a harbor hangout and sitting for hours talking. It is part of the joy of cruising.

We are not here to tell you what to do. We show people what's out there. We show them what safety gear is available, and everyone has the right to do what the hell they want.

and I wanna go sailing. . . .